Non-Alcoholic

THE
ESPRESSO BARTENDERS
GUIDE
TO
ESPRESSO BARTENDING

Over 600 Detailed Recipes

for making espresso, lattes, mochas, cappuccinos, Americanos, Italian sodas, granitas, homestyle granitas, teas, herbal teas, flavored tea drinks and more...

UPDATED REVISED EDITION

by
Sally Ann & Dara Di

D1021650

Published by Sally Ann's Hooked On Espresso

Copyright © 1994, by Sally Ann Slankard & Dara Diane Slankard

Cover design by Jerry Smith. Back cover by Dara Diane and Jerry Smith. Unless otherwise noted, illustrations sketched by Jerry Smith. Edited and typeset by Dara Diane. The Ugly Duck Bean, Three Muskateas and Herbal Teana created by Dara Diane, and sketched by Lynda Faye. Format and layout by Art Works, Woodinville, WA. Printed by Snohomish Publishing Company, Snohomish, WA.

The authors are proud that the flavor combinations are of their own creations and have sampled each and everyone. Every effort has been made to include only recipes that they developed. Should any recipe be similar to that of other publications, it is without their knowledge and is unintentional. Some trivia suggestions are presented as topics of interest and are not intended to replace recommendations by a health proffessional.

Printed in the U.S.A.

ISBN # 0-9636173-7-0

DEDICATION

Owning and operating a public service business requires long hours and true dedication. This book is for those who know the meaning of a hard days work!

And to the young entrepreneur wanna be's!

ACKNOWLEDGEMENTS

A very special thanks goes to Marie Forney, who helped me put together my first espresso recipe guide. Without that first book, there would not have been this revised edtion.

My daughter Dara, for giving up so many of her hours, days and nights, helping me to update and revise this edition.

My sister Lynda Faye, while under great pressures and a very tight schedule, interpreted and sketched, The Ugly Duck Bean, The Three Muskateas and Herbal Teana.

To Jerry Smith for his illustrations, and coming through with a great new cover design.

Many thanks to Robyn and Linda at Art Works, for their professional advice, guidance and additional editing, making this a job well done!

To the thousands who are using my original espresso recipe guide as their bible. THANK YOU!

And of course, a very special thanks to those who always look forward to Sally Ann's Super Special of the day.

Again, Thanks. This has been fun!

FORWARD

Sally Ann, is currently the owner of a very successful wholesale, retail, and mail order business. And with the help of her husband still operates her espresso bar, Hooked On Espresso.

While looking forward to opening her first espresso bar, she anticipated a book to teach her how to make the espresso drinks. With her love for cook books, she was shocked that there was none, nothing as to a basic recipe guide to get her started. Sally Ann then realized that there was a need too be fulfilled. On her own, she created recipes and wrote The Espresso Bartenders Guide To Espresso Bartending, the first of its kind! Setting the standard for mixing, measuring and adding the Italian style syrups to the espresso drinks. Since then, Sally Ann has been featured in numerous videos, news programs, a commercial and also as a guest speaker at training seminars. She still travels to trade shows promoting her books and to keep up with the latest in the espresso industry. Her books are now being sold world wide.

Sally Ann's self-publications have been the original Espresso Bartenders Guide To Espresso Bartending and Espresso Humor of the 90's. Along with the help of her daughter, using the latest products available, they completely updated and revised the original Espresso Guide, adding new recipes and incorporating tea and granita drinks. Making this truely a one stop recipe book for home and commercial use!

TABLE OF CONTENTS

SEATTLE STYLE ESPRESSO

The new age coffee drink

> 1 shot of espresso
> Romanced with steamed & frothed milk
> A little flavor added
> Topped with whipped cream and garnished.

Served at convenient locations during a time when moods and habits were ready for a change. From this trend developed the new age coffee drinks, lattés, mochas and more.

Seattle Style Glossary

Seattle seems to have its own dialect when it comes to ordering an espresso drink.

Amalfis: An Italian soda with the Half and Half floated on top.

Beef it up: Another way of saying, add a shot of espresso to my coffee.

Cher sugar: Pack of equal.

Coffee sludge: Straight or multiple shots of espresso.

Cremosa: An Italian soda with the Half and Half blended in. Same as an Italian cream soda.

Double: Used to describe how many shots of espresso one wants in their drink. (Two shots)

Double No-Fun: A non-fat latté made with two shots of decaf espresso.

Double Tall Half Caf: A 12 oz. latté made with one shot of decaf plus one shot of caffeinated espresso.

Double Tall Skinny: A 12 oz. latté made with non-fat milk and two shots of espresso.

Double Tall Two: A 12 oz. latté made with 2% milk and two shots of espresso.

Double Tall Whipless: A tall mocha made with two shots of espresso, and no whipped cream.

Flat Latté: Latté with no foam.

Flavored Moo: Steamed milk flavored with an Italian style syrup. Same as a Steamer.

Granita: A semi-frozen, slushy type drink. Dispensed from the granitore machine.

Herbal Espresso: Herbs, grains, nuts and fruits finely ground and brewed the same as espresso. Used to make espresso type drinks but contains no caffeine.

Italian Soda: Flavored syrup combined with ice and club soda.

Italian Smoothie: A version of the Italian cream soda that has been crushed with ice in a blender.

Latteccino: A cross between a latté and a cappuccino.

Leaded: Term for caffeinated.

Mocha Sludge: Straight shot of espresso flavored with chocolate syrup and topped with whipped cream.

NFL-No Score:	Non-fat latté made with decaf.
No-Fun Americano:	An americano made with decaf.
One Pull:	Single shot of espresso.
Pink, Blue, Raw, White:	Terms used when a sweetener is requested. The color of the packet indicates which sugar or sweetener is being asked for.
Quad:	Four shots of espresso. Straight or added to a drink of choice. Quad Americano, an americano made with 4 shots. This could be served in any size cup, Short, Tall or Grande.
Red Eye:	When a shot of espresso has been added to a regular cup of coffee.
Sizes:	**Short:** Term used to describe an 8 oz. cup.
	Tall: Term used to describe a 12 oz. cup.
	Grande: Term used to describe a 16 oz. cup.
Slammed:	Period when a barista has been very busy.
Split Shot:	A drink made with one total shot of espresso, only the shot of espresso would be 1/2 decaf & 1/2 caffeinated.
Steamer:	Steamed milk flavored with an Italian style syrup. Same as a Moo.
Sweet Nothing:	Decaf latté made with non-fat milk, and sweetened with artificial sweetener.
Tall Unleaded:	A 12 oz. latté made with a shot of decaf espresso.
Two Pulls:	Two shots of espresso (double.)
Unleaded:	Term for decaf.
Upside Down:	Latté made in reverse. Pour the steamed milk in the cup, top with foam, then pour the shot of espresso into the milk.

GLOSSARY

Americano: A serving of espresso, diluted with hot water to make a full cup of great tasting coffee.

Caffe Breve: Latté made with steamed Half and Half, rich and heavenly. (Heaven in a cup)

Caffe Latté: A serving of espresso with steamed milk, topped with a small amount of foam.

Cappuccino: A serving of espresso with equal parts of steamed milk and foam (wet). A serving of espresso with all foam (dry).

Con panna: Straight shot of espresso topped with whipped cream.

Crema: The dense, golden foam that forms on the top of a fresh shot of espresso.

Espresso: According to Webster's New World dictionary, espresso is defined as "coffee prepared in a special machine from finely ground coffee beans, through which steam under high pressure is forced."

Espresso Doppio: Two shots of espresso, stopped short, served in a 4 ounce portion cup.

Espresso Romano: A straight shot of espresso served with fresh lemon peel or slice of lemon. An American custom.

Flavored Latté: A 12-oz. latté flavored with 1 ounce of flavor (cherry, vanilla etc.) Sizes vary.

Flavored milk: Steamed milk (about 135°-140°) with 1 ounce of flavor added.

Frothed milk: Thick velvet, foamy milk. Before the foam and milk have had time to separate.

Flavored steamed milk: Steamed milk (about 135°-140°) with a flavor added.

Italian soda: Flavored syrup combined with ice and club soda.

Lungo: A straight shot of espresso diluted with hot water to produce a milder, or long shot of espresso. Served in a 4-ounce cup.

Mocha: A latté flavored with chocolate syrup topped with whipped cream.

Macchiato: A serving of espresso topped with a spoonful of thick velvet foam.

Non-fat Latté: A latté made with skim or non-fat milk.

Steamed milk: Milk steamed to about 135°-140°. There's something nice about a glass of warm milk.

How To Create
A Perfect Shot

Start with clean equipment.

Good water. The quality of water is an important factor to good espresso.

Preheat filter holder, brew head, shot pitcher and cup.

Use only fresh coffee beans for the grind.

Grind only the amount needed.

Check or change the grind setting throughout the day. The grind you ended with the night before may not be what you should start with in the morning. Especially if you're outdoors.

Tamp grind firmly inside basket.

Wipe excess grind off rim of group basket before inserting into brew head.

Begin your shot.

Liquid should flow evenly taking approximately 18 to 25 seconds to complete the shot (More liquid does not mean more flavor. Over extraction produces a bitter taste.)

A shot of espresso measures between 1 to 1 3/4 oz., and is topped with a rich golden crema. End your pour when you note a change in the color. A light or white color indicates that the extraction is done. The quality of the crema is your reminder of how well you did, a poor shot should never be used.

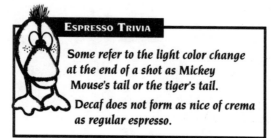

ESPRESSO TRIVIA

Some refer to the light color change at the end of a shot as Mickey Mouse's tail or the tiger's tail.

Decaf does not form as nice of crema as regular espresso.

TROUBLESHOOTING

What causes the shot to extract too quickly?
1. Not enough coffee.
2. Not tamped tightly.
3. The grind may be too coarse.
4. The grind may be too old.
5. The beans may be too old.
6. Water not at the correct brewing temperature.

Why is the shot extracting slowly?
1. Coffee tamped too tightly.
2. The grind may be too fine.
3. Too much coffee in the coffee basket.

Why is my latte tasting "green" and "bitter"?
1. Old coffee beans.
2. Over-extracted the grind.
3. Equipment not clean.
4. Grind stones need to be replaced.

Why is my shot of espresso looking watery and with poor crema?
1. Check you water temperature. (195° F)
2. Did you preheat you porta filter & shot pitchers?
3. The beans may be too old.
4. The grind may be too old.
5. The grind may be too coarse.
6. Grind stones need replacing.

Why is my flavored latte curdling?
1. Milk steamed too hot. Keep temperature just below 150 degrees.
2. Flavor goes in first, some flavors may curdle if added later, such as hazelnut and vanilla.

HELPFUL HINTS

Coffee grinds are very messy! For easy clean up, set the grinder on a tray lined with paper towels.

A pastry brush works well for brushing up coffee grinds.

Fresh brewed espresso looses its flavor within minutes of being brewed.

How fresh is your shot? When in doubt, throw it out!

Decaf does not form as nice of crema as regular espresso.

Use the top your espresso machine to keep the cups warm.

Roasted coffee beans begin to lose their flavor within one week of being roasted.

Consider using white bar towels, they bleach and sanitize nicely, Some baristas like to use two bar towels, one for the steam wand and one to wipe up spills.

ESPRESSO TRIVIA

The romance between espresso and steamed milk is fast becoming The American drink of the 90's.

Many of our grandparents and great grandparents roasted their own coffee beans at home in their ovens.

Coffee beans are usually roasted at temperatures between 400° and 425° for up to 20 minutes, depending on how dark the roast.

BREWING & STEAMING TIPS

For steaming, frothing and foaming the milk.

1. Fill the "cold" steam pitcher a little more than 1/3 full with cold milk. (Hint: non-fat, 1% and 2% foam the best.)

1.

2. Bleed the steam wand of any moisture before inserting it into the milk.

3. Now insert the tip of the steam nozzle into the milk. Open the steam valve completely to start the steaming action.

4. Tilt and lower the pitcher until the tip of the steam wand is barely under the surface of the milk. There will be a whirlpool effect, but without big bubbles, and a smooth hissing sound is heard. If the nozzle is too deep, there will be a dull rumple, and you will only be heating the milk, not creating foam.

**3.
& 4.**

5. Let the foam build. Keeping the tip of the nozzle just barely under the surface until this foaming action has expanded the quantity of milk that you started with to fill the pitcher to about 3/4 full.

5.

6. Now drop the tip of the steam nozzle down into the center to finish heating the milk.

7. Let the pitcher of steamed/foamed milk set while you make your shots of espresso. This will give the foam time to settle.

6.

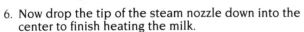

HELPFUL HINTS & TRIVIA

Moisture build up in the steam wand can slow down the foaming action.

The unique sound of the steam wand is music to a latté lovers ears!

Unscramble Seattle and what do you get?   Seattle . . . Lattes

Latté

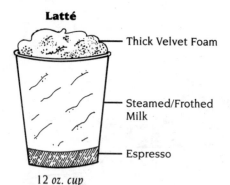

Thick Velvet Foam

Steamed/Frothed Milk

Espresso

12 oz. cup

For a latte, with a spoon, hold the foam back and pour the steamed milk into the cup over the shot of espresso. Then top it off with a small amount of foam (about a 1/2" of foam.)

Wet Cappuccino

Thick Velvet Foam

Steamed Milk

Espresso "1 shot"

12 oz. cup

For a wet cappuccino, add an equal amount of milk with the shot of espresso then top it off by filling the rest of the cup with foam. Portions will vary depending on cup size and how many "shots" of espresso are used. After adding the espresso, fill remainder of cup, 1/2 with steamed milk, 1/2 with foam.

Dry Cappuccino

Thick Velvet Foam

Espresso

12 oz. cup

For a dry cappuccino, with a spoon, scoop out the thick, dense foam and put it over the shot of espresso, filling the cup.

If it's a good"n"dry cappuccino, you'll be able to stand an ice teaspoon in it, and the spoon won't fall over (12 oz. cup.)

8

HELPFUL HINTS

Caution: When heat testing a steam pitcher, lotion on your hands will falsify the temperature.

After each steaming, immediately wipe clean your steam wand.

Keep your milk fresh, clean the steam pitchers about every two hours. Its wise to have extra steam pitchers on hand.

When in a large size cup, a latté made with one shot of espresso can taste very milky. For a more coffee taste simply increase the amount of espresso.

Leftover steamed milk can be refrothed by combining it with fresh "cold" milk. Refrigerate between steamings.

For quality foam, froth fresh "cold" milk in a "cold" stainless steel steaming pitcher.

If your frothed milk looks like you blew through a straw to create the foam, your bubbles are too big. Try again.

A spoon in the pitcher while steaming, helps to prevent the milk from scorching.

For dense foam, while frothing the milk, agitate and break the bubbles up with a spoon.

For safe temperature control, use a candy thermometer that attaches to the side of the steam pitcher.

GUIDELINE STEAMING TEMPERATURES

Steam brevés and egg nog to 145°

Steam lattés to 150°

Steam mochas to 150°-155°

Some flavors may curdle when hot milk is added to them. Steam the milk to about 135°-145°

MILK TYPES & PRODUCTS

- Nonfat
- 1% fat
- 2% fat
- Whole milk
- Half N Half
- Whipped cream
- Egg Nog
- Non-dairy (*soy based creamers*)
- Acidophilus lowfat milk
- Lactaid nonfat milk
- Pre-flavored milk

All these milk types can be heated and steamed for making the espresso drinks. Some just simply foam better than others.

TERMS FOR HEATING & STEAMING THE MILK

Steamed milk: Milk that has been heated, with the steam wand held close to the bottom of the pitcher. (steaming method) With no attention being paid to the creating of foam.

Frothed milk: Milk that has been carefully steamed and expanded to create a condensed velvet foam, and the foam has not yet separated from the milk.

Foamed milk: Milk that has been carefully steamed, and has expanded. (same as for the frothed milk) But when allowed to set, the foam rises and settles at the top of the milk. Allowing it to be scooped out by a spoon.

Pre-flavored steamed milk: You can steam pre-flavored milk or you can create a flavor of your own. Simply, add 1 ounce of an Italian style syrup (any flavor) to 1/3 pitcher of cold milk (follow the steaming methods) You will then have a lightly flavored steamed milk with very tasty foam, for making lattes or drinking as is.

FOR VARIATIONS WITH THE FLAVORED STEAMED MILK

In a 12 oz. cup add:

    1/2 oz.   Flavored Italian style syrup (vanilla)
    1 shot   Espresso

While holding back the foam, pour in a flavored steamed milk (cherry), and top it off with the flavored foam.

NEAPOLITAN'S CAPPUCCINO

In three different pitchers steam one with creme de cacao Italian style syrup, one with coconut Italian style syrup, and one with orange Italian style syrup. Let the pitchers of steamed milk set, allowing the foam to settle to the top. Then layer the thick foam gently in a 12 oz. cup, 1/3 creme de cacao, 1/3 coconut, and 1/3 orange. Now gently pour one shot of espresso over the foam. YUM!

This is a fun method and you can create many variations, but you should wash and rinse the steam pitchers after each use.

FUN TOPPINGS AND GARNISHES

Almond powder
Brown sugar
Candy canes
Chocolate brown sugar shakeable topping
Chocolate candy sprinkles
Chocolate covered espresso beans (white or dark)
Chocolate powder (unsweetened)
Cinnamon
Cinnamon brown sugar shakeable topping
Cinnamon sticks
Colorful candy sprinkles
Crushed cookies (oreos etc...)
Dried fruits (Banana slices, pineapple, cherries etc...)
Flavored whipped cream
Fruit slices
Fruit kabobs
Fruit syrups drizzled lightly over drinks
Foam
Grated bitter chocolate
Grated Mexican chocolate
Grated orange or lemon rind
Maraschino cherries
Mini-marshmellows
Mini candy bars
Mini cookies
Nutmeg
Nutmeg brown sugar shakeable topping
Nuts (whole or crushed)
Raspberry shakeable topping granules
Raw sugar
Shaved chocolate
Toasted coconut
Whipped cream
Vanilla powder

MEASUREMENTS

Measuring does not need to be difficult or does it need to be exact. After all, this is not a chemistry class, there are no teachers to grade you. But then, customer satisfaction is important, so you should be close.

The 12 oz. cup is the most popular size, and once you learn to add flavors to this size, it will then be easy to adjust the syrup amounts to other size cups.

Most of the syrup combinations are based on a total of 1 ounce of flavor to a 12 ounce espresso drink.

Example: 1/2 oz. Cherry syrup + 1/2 oz. Vanilla syrup = 1 oz.

Remember, tastes vary, so at times you may need to adjust the flavor amount.

BASIC MEASUREMENT GUIDELINES

For hot espresso based drinks

> 8 oz. cup - 1/2 oz. flavor
> 12 oz. cup - 1 oz. flavor
> 16 oz. cup - 1 1/2 oz. flavor

EASY GUIDELINE FOR ADDING FLAVORS

12 oz. cup

Whipped Cream & Garnish (5)

Steamed Milk (4)

(3) Blend Well

Espresso (2)
Flavor (1)

For best results combine in order given. Blend before adding topping.

MEASUREMENT EQUIPMENT

Measuring Spoons
3 tsp. = 1 tbsp.
2 tbsp. = 1 oz.

**Shot glass that
indicates the ounces.**

**Clear measuring cup that is
marked in ounces.**

Pump
Some pumps measure out 1 oz.
of syrup per pump. Check the
amount your pump dispenses.

**Learn to eyeball
your measurements.**

2 quart pitcher

Ice Cube Tray
The ice cube trays that we used
made 14, 1 oz. ice cubes. It
helps to know how much
liquid that your ice
cube tray holds.

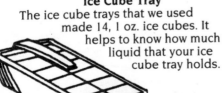

NEW PRODUCTS

Working with new products can be fun and easy. Go for it. Here are some simple recipe guidelines to help get you started.

NEW PRODUCT GUIDELINE

Working with a new Italian style syrup
• •

(based on a 12 oz. cup)

1 oz.	New flavor Italian style syrup
1 shot	Espresso
	Steamed milk

Pour 1 oz. of the new syrup into a 12 oz. cup. Add espresso and steamed milk. Top with whipped cream and garnish.

Combining two syrups, new or old
• •

Start with a 1/2 ounce of each flavor.

Example

(12 oz. cup)

1/2 oz.	Black cherry Italian style syrup
1/2 oz.	Almond Italian style syrup
	(1 oz. Total of Italian style syrup for this cup size.)
1 shot	Espresso
	Steamed milk

Pour syrups into the cup, add the espresso and steamed milk. Stir, add whipped cream and garnish.

Does one flavor seem to be more dominant in taste? If so, try this combination.
• •

Example

(12 oz. cup)

3/4 oz.	Black cherry Italian style syrup (less dominate)
1/4 oz.	Almond Italian style syrup (dominate)
	(1 oz. Total of Italian style syrup for this cup size.)
1 shot	Espresso
	Steamed milk

Pour syrups into the cup, add the espresso and steamed milk. Stir, add whipped cream and garnish.

Working with powdered pre-packaged instant flavor drink mixes.

(instant flavored coffees, gourmet hot cocoa mixes, instant flavored milk and egg nog drinks, etc. Many of these pre-packaged drink mixes contain powdered milk, or non-dairy creamers. So when adding steamed milk consider using non-fat or 2%, or just hot water.)

When mixing, follow the manufacturers instructions, but leave enough room in the cup for one shot of espresso. (most of these pre-packaged mixes are designed for an 8 oz. cup.)

EXAMPLES

Cafe Vienna

(8 oz. cup)

1	Package Cafe Vienna instant coffee mix
1 shot	Espresso
	Steamed milk

In an 8 oz. cup, dissolve the instant coffee mix with a shot of espresso. Fill the remainder of the cup with steamed milk. Add whipped cream and garnish.

White Chocolate Mocha

(8 oz. cup)

1 package	Instant White Chocolate drink mix
1 shot	Espresso
	Steamed milk

In an 8 oz. cup dissolve the White Chocolate mix with the espresso. Fill the remainder of the cup with steamed milk. Add whipped cream and garnish.

Egg Nog

(8 oz. cup)

1 package	Instant powdered egg nog drink mix
1 shot	Espresso
	Steamed milk

In an 8 oz. cup, dissolve the powdered egg nog mix with the espresso. Fill remainder of cup with steamed milk. Add whipped cream and garnish.

The following are recipes that are based on the 3 previous instant drink mixes. But here we've recreated them, by flavoring them with an Italian style syrup. (**NOTE: We've increased the size to a 12 oz. cup.**)

Cafe Vienna and Cinnamon

(12 *oz. cup*)

1 package	Cafe Vienna instant coffee drink mix
1/2 oz.	Cinnamon Italian style syrup
1 shot	Espresso
	Steamed milk

In a 12 oz. cup add the cinnamon Italian style syrup, Cafe Vienna instant coffee mix, and dissolve with the espresso. Fill the remainder of the cup with steamed milk. Add whipped cream and dust with cinnamon.

Raspberry Nougat Latte

(12 *oz. cup*)

1 package	Instant White Chocolate drink mix
1/2 oz.	Raspberry Italian style syrup
1 shot	Espresso
	Steamed milk

In a 12 oz. cup add the raspberry Italian style syrup, instant white chocolate drink mix and dissolve with the espresso. Fill the remainder of the cup with steamed milk. Add whipped cream, drizzle with walnut Italian style syrup, and garnish with chocolate sprinkles.

Egg Nog Deluxe Latte

(12 *oz. cup*)

1 package	Instant powdered eggnog drink mix
1 oz.	Eggnog Italian style syrup
1 shot	Espresso
	Steamed milk

In a 12 oz. cup add the egg nog Italian style syrup, instant powdered egg nog drink mix, and dissolve with the espresso. Fill the remainder of the cup with steamed milk. Add whipped cream and dust with nutmeg.

ESPRESSO

● ●

Straight Shots & Flavored Shots

According to Webster's New World dictionary, espresso is defined as "coffee prepared in a special machine from finely ground coffee beans, through which steam under high pressure is forced." This method takes 18 to 25 seconds, giving way to the meaning express or fast.

A straight shot of espresso measures between 1 to 1 3/4 oz. and is topped with a deep golden crema. A straight shot of espresso should always be poured/brewed directly into the cup in which it is being served.

Shot of Espresso

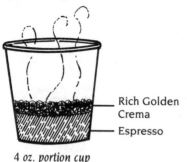

Rich Golden Crema
Espresso

4 oz. portion cup

Flavored Shot of Espresso

Thick Velvet Foam or Topping of Choice

Espresso
Flavor

4 oz. portion cup

STRAIGHT SHOT RECIPES

Chocolate Espresso (mocha sludge)

Brew one shot of espresso directly into a 4 oz. portion cup, add 1/2 oz. chocolate syrup. Blend. Top with whipped cream, and dust with chocolate powder.

Con Ponna

Brew one shot of espresso directly into a 4 oz. portion cup. Top with whipped cream.

Date Nut Espresso

Brew one shot of espresso directly into a 4 oz. portion cup, add 1/4 oz. tamarindo Italian style syrup, 1/4 oz. walnut Italian style syrup. Blend. Top with thick velvet foam made from Half and Half.

Espresso De Borgia

Brew one shot of espresso directly into a 4 oz. portion cup, add 1/2 oz. creme de cacao Italian style syrup, 1/4 oz. amaretto Italian style syrup. Blend. Top with whipped cream, and a dash of nutmeg.

Espresso Macchiato

Brew one shot of espresso directly into a 4 oz. portion cup. Top with 1 to 2 table-spoons of frothed milk.

Mocha Espresso Cream

Brew one shot of espresso directly into a 4 oz. portion cup, add 1/2 oz. chocolate syrup. Blend. Fill remainder of cup with steamed Half and Half. Top with whipped cream.

Quad Straight

A serving of four shots of espresso in an 8 oz. cup.

Raspberry Espresso Cream

Brew one shot of espresso directly into a 4 oz. portion cup, add 1/2 oz. raspberry Italian style syrup. Blend. Fill remainder of cup with steamed Half and Half. Top with whipped cream.

ESPRESSO TRUFFLES

Butterscotch Espresso Truffle

In a 8 oz. cup combine:
- 1/2 oz. Butterscotch topping
- 1 shot Espresso

Blend well, let cool for 1 minute. Fill cup 3/4 full with whipped cream. Whip ingredients together until thick and fluffy. Top with whipped cream, and dust with chocolate powder.

Caramel Nut Espresso Truffle

In a 8 oz. cup combine:
- 1/2 oz. Caramel topping
- 1 shot Espresso

Blend well, let cool for 1 minute. Fill cup 3/4 full with whipped cream. Whip ingredients together until thick and fluffy. Top with whipped cream, and drizzle with hazelnut Italian style syrup.

Caramel Espresso Truffle Delight

In a 8 oz. cup combine:
- 1/2 oz. Caramel topping
- 1 shot Espresso

Blend well, let cool for 1 minute. Fill cup 3/4 full with whipped cream. Whip ingredients together until thick and fluffy. Top with whipped cream.

Dark Chocolate Nut Espresso Truffle

In a 8 oz. cup combine:

1/2 oz.	Bittersweet chocolate
1/4 oz.	Walnut Italian style syrup
1 shot	Espresso

Blend well, let cool for 1 minute. Fill cup 3/4 full with whipped cream. Whip ingredients together until thick and fluffy. Top with whipped cream, and dust with chocolate powder.

Mocha Fudge Espresso Truffle

In a 8 oz. cup combine:

1/2 oz.	Chocolate fudge topping
1 shot	Espresso

Blend well, let cool for 1 minute. Fill cup 3/4 full with whipped cream. Whip ingredients together until thick and fluffy. Top with whipped cream, and garnish with a chocolate covered espresso bean.

White Chocolate Espresso Truffle

In a 8 oz. cup combine:

3/4 oz.	White chocolate base (see page 121)
1 shot	Espresso

Blend well, let cool for 1 minute. Fill cup 3/4 full with whipped cream. Whip ingredients together until thick and fluffy. Top with whipped cream, and drizzle lightly with raspberry Italian style syrup.

ESPRESSO TRIVIA

It's true! A shot of espresso has less caffeine than a cup of drip coffee.

Whats Mach 1? The first time you ever tried a straight shot - straight to the trash can!

What is coffee sludge? A straight shot of espresso.

AMERICANOS

Americano

Half and Half *optional*

Hot Water

Espresso

12 oz. cup

Flavored Americano

Topping

Hot Water

Espresso
Flavor

12 oz. cup

Americano

In a 12 oz. cup combine:

    1 shot   Espresso
    Hot water   Enough to fill cup.

Like a regular cup of coffee, you can add Half and Half and sweeten.

Almond de Cacao Americano

In a 12 oz. cup combine:

    1/2 oz.   Almond Italian style syrup
    1/2 oz.   Creme de cacao Italian style syrup
    1 shot   Espresso
    Hot water   Enough to fill cup.

Add Half and Half if desired.

Amaretto Americano

In a 12 oz. cup combine:

    3/4 oz.   Amaretto Italian style syrup
    1 shot   Espresso
    Hot water   Enough to fill cup.

Add Half and Half if desired.

Apple Americano

In a 12 oz. cup combine:

    1/2 oz.   Apple Italian style syrup
    1/2 oz.   Praline Italian style syrup
    1 shot   Espresso
    Hot water   Enough to fill cup.

Stir with cinnamon stick.

Bahamian Rumba Americano

In a 12 oz. cup combine:

1/2 oz.	Praline Italian style syrup
1/2 oz.	Rum Italian style syrup
1 shot	Espresso
Hot water	Enough to fill cup.

Top with whipped cream.

Bavarian Mint Americano

In a 12 oz. cup combine:

1/2 oz.	Coffee Italian style syrup
1/2 oz.	Chocolate mint Italian style syrup
1 shot	Espresso
Hot water	Enough to fill cup.

Top with whipped cream, and drizzle with chocolate syrup.

Cafe Au Chocolate Americano

In a 12 oz. cup combine:

1 oz.	Chocolate syrup
1 shot	Espresso
Hot water	Enough to fill cup.

Top with whipped cream, and dust with cinnamon.

Cherry Jubilee Americano

In a 12 oz. cup combine:

1/2 oz.	Cherry Italian style syrup
1/4 oz.	Vanilla Italian style syrup
1/4 oz.	Cinnamon Italian style syrup
1 shot	Espresso
Hot water	Enough to fill cup 3/4 full.

Add 1 oz. Half and Half, and top with whipped cream.

Coconut Cream Americano

In a 12 oz. cup combine:

1 oz.	Coconut Italian style syrup
1 shot	Espresso
Hot water	Enough to fill cup 3/4 full.

Add 1 oz. Half and Half, and top with whipped cream.

Coconut De Cacao Americano

In a 12 oz. cup combine:

1/2 oz.	Coconut Italian style syrup
1/2 oz.	Creme de cacao Italian style syrup
1 shot	Espresso
Hot water	Enough to fill cup.

Top with whipped cream.

Coffee Americano

In a 12 oz. cup combine:

1 oz.	Coffee Italian style syrup
1 shot	Espresso
Hot water	Enough to fill cup.

Top with whipped cream.

Hazelnut Truffle Americano

In a 12 oz. cup combine:

1/2 oz.	Hazelnut Italian style syrup
1/2 oz.	Chocolate syrup
1 shot	Espresso
Hot water	Enough to fill cup.

Top with whipped cream.

Irish Cream Americano

In a 12 oz. cup combine:

1 oz.	Irish cream Italian style syrup
1 shot	Espresso
Hot water	Enough to fill cup 3/4 full.

Add 1 oz. Half and Half, and top with whipped cream.

Jamaican Style Americano

In a 12 oz. cup combine:

1/2 oz.	Coffee Italian style syrup
1/2 oz.	Rum Italian style syrup
1 shot	Espresso
Hot water	Enough to fill cup.

Top with whipped cream.

Maple Nut Americano

In a 12 oz. cup combine:

1/2 oz.	Pure maple syrup
1/2 oz.	Hazelnut Italian style syrup
1 shot	Espresso
Hot water	Enough to fill cup.

Top with whipped cream.

Mexican Americano

In a 12 oz. cup combine:

1 oz.	Mexican chocolate powder
1/4 oz.	Almond Italian style syrup
1 shot	Espresso
Hot water	Enough to fill cup.

Top with whipped cream.

Orange Americano

In a 12 oz. cup combine:

1 oz.	Orange Italian style syrup
1 shot	Espresso
Hot water	Enough to fill cup.

Add 1 oz. Half and Half if desired.

Raspberry Cream Americano

In a 12 oz. cup combine:

1 oz.	Raspberry Italian style syrup
1 shot	Espresso
Hot water	Enough to fill cup 3/4 full.

Add 1 oz. Half and Half, and top with whipped cream.

Rum Americano

In a 12 oz. cup combine:

1 oz.	Rum Italian style syrup
1 shot	Espresso
Hot water	Enough to fill cup.

Vanilla Americano

In a 12 oz. cup combine:

1 oz.	Vanilla Italian style syrup
1 shot	Espresso
Hot water	Enough to fill cup.

White Chocolate Americano

In a 12 oz. cup combine:

1 oz.	White chocolate
1 shot	Espresso
Hot water	Enough to fill cup.

HELPFUL HINTS

A professional coffee taster is called a "cupper."

An Americano is simply an excellent cup of coffee!

Americanos should be cooled slightly with cold water or milk, ice or cream.

Its also best to double cup an Americano drink.

BASIC LATTÉ COMBINATIONS

Latté

Thick Velvet Foam

Steamed/ Frothed Milk

Espresso

12 oz. cup

Flavored Latté

Whipped Cream & Garnish

Steamed Milk

Espresso
Flavor

12 oz. cup

Almond Latté

In a 12 oz. cup combine:

3/4 oz.	Almond Italian style syrup
1 shot	Espresso
	Steamed milk of choice.

Blend. Top with whipped cream, and dust with powdered almond.

Almond Bark Latté

In a 12 oz. cup combine:

1/2 oz.	Almond Italian style syrup
1/2 oz.	White chocolate
1 shot	Espresso
	Steamed milk of choice.

Blend. Top with whipped cream, and dust with powdered almond.

Almond Fudge Latté

In a 12 oz. cup combine:

1/2 oz.	Almond Italian style syrup
1/2 oz.	Chocolate fudge Italian style syrup
1 shot	Espresso
	Steamed milk of choice.

Blend. Top with whipped cream, and drizzle with chocolate syrup.

Amaretto Latté

In a 12 oz. cup combine:

3/4 oz.	Amaretto Italian style syrup
1 shot	Espresso
	Steamed milk of choice.

Blend. Top with amaretto or plain whipped cream.

Amaretto Fudge Latté

In a 12 oz. cup combine:

- 1/2 oz.   Amaretto Italian style syrup
- 1/2 oz.   Chocolate fudge Italian style syrup
- 1 shot   Espresso
- Steamed milk of choice.

Blend. Top with amaretto whipped cream, and drizzle with a small amount of the chocolate syrup.

Anisette Latté

In a 12 oz. cup combine:

- 1 oz.   Anisette Italian style syrup
- 1 shot   Espresso
- Steamed milk of choice.

Blend. Top with whipped cream, and garnish with licorice candy.

Anisette & Strawberry Latté

In a 12 oz. cup combine:

- 3/4 oz.   Strawberry Italian style syrup
- 1/4 oz.   Anisette Italian style syrup
- 1 shot   Espresso
- Steamed milk of choice.

Blend. Top with whipped cream, drizzle a small amount of the strawberry syrup.

Almond & Creme de Cassis Latté

In a 12 oz. cup combine:

- 3/4 oz.   Almond Italian style syrup
- 1/4 oz.   Creme de cassis Italian style syrup
- 1 shot   Espresso
- Steamed milk of choice.

Blend. Top with whipped cream.

Apple Latté

In a 12 oz. cup combine:

- 1 oz.   Apple Italian style syrup
- 1 shot   Espresso
- Steamed milk of choice.

Blend. Top with a flavored or plain whipped cream, and dust with nutmeg.

Apple Strawberry Latté

In a 12 oz. cup combine:

    1/2 oz. Apple Italian style syrup
    1/2 oz. Strawberry Italian style syrup
    1 shot Espresso
             Steamed milk of choice.

Blend. Top with strawberry flavored whipped cream, and dust with cinnamon.

Apple Walnut Latté

In a 12 oz. cup combine:

    1/2 oz. Apple Italian style syrup
    1/2 oz. Walnut Italian style syrup
    1 shot Espresso
             Steamed milk of choice.

Blend. Top with whipped cream, and dust with cinnamon.

Banana Latté

In a 12 oz. cup combine:

    3/4 oz. Banana Italian style syrup
    1 shot Espresso
             Steamed milk of choice.

Blend. Top with strawberry flavored whipped cream.

Banana Nut Latté

In a 12 oz. cup combine:

    3/4 oz. Banana Italian style syrup
    1/4 oz. Hazelnut Italian style syrup
    1 shot Espresso
             Steamed milk of choice.

Blend. Top with whipped cream, and dust with cinnamon and brown sugar.

Banana Walnut Latté

In a 12 oz. cup combine:

    1/2 oz. Banana Italian style syrup
    1/2 oz. Walnut Italian style syrup
    1 shot Espresso
             Steamed milk of choice.

Blend. Top with whipped cream, and dust with cinnamon.

Banana Coconut Latté

In a 12 oz. cup combine:

1/2 oz.	Banana Italian style syrup
1/2 oz.	Coconut Italian style syrup
1 shot	Espresso
	Steamed milk of choice.

Blend. Top with whipped cream, and garnish with toasted coconut.

Banana Chocolate Fudge Latté

In a 12 oz. cup combine:

1/2 oz.	Banana Italian style syrup
1/2 oz.	Chocolate fudge Italian style syrup
1 shot	Espresso
	Steamed milk of choice.

Blend. Top with whipped cream, and drizzle lightly with the chocolate fudge syrup.

Bavarian Chocolate Latté

In a 12 oz. cup combine:

1 oz.	Bavarian chocolate Italian style syrup
1 shot	Espresso
	Steamed milk of choice.

Blend. Top with whipped cream, and sprinkle with chocolate-brown sugar granules.

Bavarian Mint Latté

In a 12 oz. cup combine:

1/2 oz.	Coffee Italian style syrup
1/2 oz.	Chocolate mint Italian style syrup
1 shot	Espresso
	Steamed milk of choice.

Blend. Top with whipped cream, and garnish with bits of shaved chocolate.

Bing Cherry Latté

In a 12 oz. cup combine:

1 oz.	Bing cherry Italian style syrup
1 shot	Espresso
	Steamed milk of choice.

Blend. Top with whipped cream.

Bing Cherry Vanilla Latté

In a 12 oz. cup combine:

1/2 oz.	Bing cherry Italian style syrup
1/2 oz.	Vanilla Italian style syrup
1 shot	Espresso
	Steamed milk of choice.

Blend. Top with whipped cream, and garnish with almond powder.

Blackberry Latté

In a 12 oz. cup combine:

3/4 oz.	Blackberry Italian style syrup
1 shot	Espresso
	Steamed milk of choice.

Blend. Top with whipped cream, and dust lightly with cinnamon.

Blackberry Banana Latté

In a 12 oz. cup combine:

1/2 oz.	Blackberry Italian style syrup
1/2 oz.	Banana Italian style syrup
1 shot	Espresso
	Steamed milk of choice

Blend. Top with whipped cream, and sprinkle with cinnamon-brown sugar granules.

Blackberry Coconut Latté

In a 12 oz. cup combine:

1/2 oz.	Blackberry Italian style syrup
1/2 oz.	Coconut Italian style syrup
1 shot	Espresso
	Steamed milk of choice.

Blend. Top with whipped cream, and dust lightly with cinnamon.

Blackberry Cherry Latté

In a 12 oz. cup combine:

1/2 oz.	Blackberry Italian style syrup
1/2 oz.	Cherry Italian style syrup
1 shot	Espresso
	Steamed milk of choice.

Blend. Top with whipped cream.

Blackberry Fudge Latté

In a 12 oz. cup combine:

1/2 oz.	Blackberry Italian style syrup
1/2 oz.	Chocolate Fudge Italian style syrup
I shot	Espresso
	Steamed milk of choice.

Blend. Top with whipped cream, and garnish with chocolate sprinkles.

Black Cherry Latté

In a 12 oz. cup combine:

1 oz.	Black cherry Italian style syrup
I shot	Espresso
	Steamed milk of choice.

Blend. Top with whipped cream.

Black Cherry Almond Latté

In a 12 oz. cup combine:

3/4 oz.	Black cherry Italian style syrup
1/4 oz.	Almond Italian style syrup
I shot	Espresso
	Steamed milk of choice.

Blend. Top with whipped cream.

Black Cherry Walnut Latté

In a 12 oz. cup combine:

1/2 oz.	Black cherry Italian style syrup
1/2 oz.	Walnut Italian style syrup
I shot	Espresso
	Steamed milk of choice.

Blend. Top with whipped cream, and dust with cinnamon.

Black Raspberry Latté

In a 12 oz. cup combine:

1 oz.	Black raspberry Italian style syrup
I shot	Espresso
	Steamed milk of choice.

Blend. Top with whipped cream, and sprinkle with raspberry sugar granules.

Blueberry Latté

In a 12 oz. cup combine:

    1 oz.   Blueberry Italian style syrup
    1 shot Espresso
            Steamed milk of choice.

Blend. Top with whipped cream.

Blueberry Almond Latté

In a 12 oz. cup combine:

    3/4 oz. Blueberry Italian style syrup
    1/4 oz. Almond Italian style syrup
    1 shot Espresso
            Steamed milk of choice.

Blend. Top with whipped cream, and dust with almond powder.

Boysenberry Latté

In a 12 oz. cup combine:

    1 oz.   Boysenberry Italian style syrup
    1 shot Espresso
            Steamed milk of choice.

Blend. Top with whipped cream.

Boysenberry Almond Latté

In a 12 oz. cup combine:

    1/2 oz. Boysenberry Italian style syrup
    1/2 oz. Almond Italian style syrup
    1 shot Espresso
            Steamed milk of choice.

Blend. Top with whipped cream.

Boysenberry Vanilla Latté

In a 12 oz. cup combine:

    1/2 oz. Boysenberry Italian style syrup
    1/2 oz. Vanilla Italian style syrup
    1 shot Espresso
            Steamed milk of choice.

Blend. Top with whipped cream.

Butter Pecan Latté

In a 12 oz. cup combine:

  1 oz.   Butter pecan Italian style syrup
  1 shot Espresso
          Steamed milk of choice.

Blend. Top with whipped cream.

Butter Pecan & Rum Latté

In a 12 oz. cup combine:

  1/2 oz. Butter pecan Italian style syrup
  1/2 oz. Rum Italian style syrup
  1 shot   Espresso
           Steamed milk of choice.

Blend. Top with whipped cream, and dust lightly with cinnamon.

Butter Rum Latté

In a 12 oz. cup combine:

  1 oz.   Butter rum Italian style syrup
  1 shot Espresso
          Steamed milk of choice.

Blend. Top with whipped cream.

Butter Rum & Coffee Latté

In a 12 oz. cup combine:

  1/2 oz. Butter rum Italian style syrup
  1/2 oz. Coffee Italian style syrup
  1 shot   Espresso
           Steamed milk of choice.

Blend. Top with whipped cream.

Butterscotch Latté

In a 12 oz. cup combine:

  1 oz.   Butterscotch Italian style syrup
  1 shot Espresso
          Steamed milk of choice.

Blend. Top with whipped cream.

Butterscotch & Creme de Cacao Latté

In a 12 oz. cup combine:

1/2 oz.	Butterscotch Italian style syrup
1/2 oz.	Creme de cacao Italian style syrup
1 shot	Espresso
	Steamed milk of choice.

Blend. Top with whipped cream, and garnish with chocolate sprinkles.

B 52 Latté

In a 12 oz. cup combine:

1 oz.	B 52 Italian style syrup
1 shot	Espresso
	Steamed milk of choice.

Blend. Top with amaretto flavored whipped cream.

Caramel Latté

In a 12 oz. cup combine:

1 oz.	Caramel Italian style syrup
1 shot	Espresso
	Steamed milk of choice.

Blend. Top with whipped cream.

Caramel Almond Latté

In a 12 oz. cup combine:

3/4 oz.	Caramel Italian style syrup
1/4 oz.	Almond Italian style syrup
1 shot	Espresso
	Steamed milk of choice.

Blend. Top with whipped cream.

Caramel Coconut Latté

In a 12 oz. cup combine:

1/2 oz.	Caramel Italian style syrup
1/2 oz.	Coconut Italian style syrup
1 shot	Espresso
	Steamed milk of choice.

Blend. Top with whipped cream.

Caramel Fudge Latté

In a 12 oz. cup combine:

1/2 oz.	Caramel Italian style syrup
1/2 oz.	Chocolate Fudge Italian style syrup
1 shot	Espresso
	Steamed milk of choice.

Blend. Top with whipped cream, and garnish with chocolate sprinkles.

Caramel Hazelnut Latté

In a 12 oz. cup combine:

3/4 oz.	Caramel Italian style syrup
1/4 oz.	Hazelnut Italian style syrup
1 shot	Espresso
	Steamed milk of choice.

Blend. Top with whipped cream.

Caramel Vanilla Latté

In a 12 oz. cup combine:

1/2 oz.	Caramel Italian style syrup
1/2 oz.	Vanilla Italian style syrup
1 shot	Espresso
	Steamed milk of choice.

Blend. Top with whipped cream.

Caramel Walnut Latté

In a 12 oz. cup combine:

1/2 oz.	Caramel Italian style syrup
1/2 oz.	Walnut Italian style syrup
1 shot	Espresso
	Steamed milk of choice.

Blend. Top with whipped cream.

Cherry Latté

In a 12 oz. cup combine:

1 oz.	Cherry Italian style syrup
1 shot	Espresso
	Steamed milk of choice.

Blend. Top with amaretto flavored whipped cream.

Cherry Almond Latté

In a 12 oz. cup combine:

- 3/4 oz. Cherry Italian style syrup
- 1/4 oz. Almond Italian style syrup
- 1 shot Espresso
- Steamed milk of choice.

Blend. Top with whipped cream, and dust with almond powder.

Cherry Banana Latté

In a 12 oz. cup combine:

- 1/2 oz. Cherry Italian style syrup
- 1/2 oz. Banana Italian style syrup
- 1 shot Espresso
- Steamed milk of choice.

Blend. Top with whipped cream.

Cherry Coconut Latté

In a 12 oz. cup combine:

- 1/2 oz. Cherry Italian style syrup
- 1/2 oz. Coconut Italian style syrup
- 1 shot Espresso
- Steamed milk of choice.

Blend. Top with whipped cream.

Cherry Vanilla Latté

In a 12 oz. cup combine:

- 1/2 oz. Cherry Italian style syrup
- 1/2 oz. Vanilla Italian style syrup
- 1 shot Espresso
- Steamed milk of choice.

Blend. Top with whipped cream, and dust with cinnamon.

Chocolate Fudge Latté

In a 12 oz. cup combine:

- 1 oz. Chocolate fudge Italian style syrup
- 1 shot Espresso
- Steamed milk of choice.

Blend. Top with whipped cream, and garnish with chocolate sprinkles.

Chocolate Mint Latté . . . .

In a 12 oz. cup combine:

    1 oz.   Chocolate mint Italian style syrup
    1 shot Espresso
             Steamed milk of choice.

Blend. Top with whipped cream, and garnish with chocolate sprinkles.

Cinnamon Latté . . . .

In a 12 oz. cup combine:

    1 oz.   Cinnamon Italian style syrup
    1 shot Espresso
             Steamed milk of choice.

Blend. Top with whipped cream, and dust with cinnamon-brown sugar granules.

Coconut Latté . . . .

In a 12 oz. cup combine:

    1 oz.   Coconut Italian style syrup
    1 shot Espresso
             Steamed milk of choice.

Blend. Top with whipped cream.

Coconut Banana Latté . . . .

In a 12 oz. cup combine:

    1/2 oz. Coconut Italian style syrup
    1/2 oz. Banana Italian style syrup
    1 shot   Espresso
              Steamed milk of choice.

Blend. Top with whipped cream.

Coconut Coffee Latté . . . .

In a 12 oz. cup combine:

    1/2 oz. Coconut Italian style syrup
    1/2 oz. Coffee Italian style syrup
    1 shot   Espresso
              Steamed milk of choice.

Blend. Top with whipped cream.

Coconut Orange Latté

In a 12 oz. cup combine:

1/2 oz.	Coconut Italian style syrup
1/2 oz.	Orange Italian style syrup
1 shot	Espresso
	Steamed milk of choice.

Blend. Top with whipped cream.

Coconut Vanilla Latté

In a 12 oz. cup combine:

1/2 oz.	Coconut Italian style syrup
1/2 oz.	Vanilla Italian style syrup
1 shot	Espresso
	Steamed milk of choice.

Blend. Top with whipped cream.

Coffee (Kahlua) Latté

In a 12 oz. cup combine:

1 oz.	Coffee syrup
1 shot	Espresso
	Steamed milk of choice.

Blend. Top with whipped cream.

Coffee & Almond Latté

In a 12 oz. cup combine:

1/4 oz.	Almond Italian style syrup
3/4 oz.	Coffee Italian style syrup
1 shot	Espresso
	Steamed milk of choice.

Blend. Top with amaretto or plain whipped cream, and dust with almond powder.

Coffee & Chocolate Mint Latté

In a 12 oz. cup combine:

1/2 oz.	Chocolate mint Italian style syrup
1/2 oz.	Coffee Italian style syrup
1 shot	Espresso
	Steamed milk of choice.

Blend. Top with whipped cream.

Coffee & Coconut Latté

In a 12 oz. cup combine:

    1/2 oz.   Coffee Italian style syrup
    1/2 oz.   Coconut Italian style syrup
    1 shot   Espresso
            Steamed milk of choice.

Blend. Top with whipped cream.

Coffee & Nut Latté

In a 12 oz. cup combine:

    3/4 oz.   Coffee Italian style syrup
    1/4 oz.   Hazelnut Italian style syrup
    1 shot   Espresso
            Steamed milk of choice.

Blend. Top with whipped cream.

Coffee & Orange Latté

In a 12 oz. cup combine:

    1/2 oz.   Coffee Italian style syrup
    1/2 oz.   Orange Italian style syrup
    1 shot   Espresso
            Steamed milk of choice.

Blend. Top with whipped cream.

Coffee & Raspberry Latté

In a 12 oz. cup combine:

    1/2 oz.   Coffee Italian style syrup
    1/2 oz.   Raspberry Italian style syrup
    1 shot   Espresso
            Steamed milk of choice.

Blend. Top with whipped cream.

Coffee & Vanilla Latté

In a 12 oz. cup combine:

    1/2 oz.   Coffee Italian style syrup
    1/2 oz.   Vanilla Italian style syrup
    1 shot   Espresso
            Steamed milk of choice.

Blend. Top with whipped cream.

Creme de Cacao Latté

In a 12 oz. cup combine:

    1 oz.   Creme de cacao Italian style syrup
    1 shot Espresso
            Steamed milk of choice.

Blend. Top with whipped cream.

Creme de Cacao & Banana Latté

In a 12 oz. cup combine:

    1/2 oz. Creme de cacao Italian style syrup
    1/2 oz. Banana Italian style syrup
    1 shot Espresso
            Steamed milk of choice.

Blend. Top with whipped cream.

Creme de Cacao & Caramel Latté

In a 12 oz. cup combine:

    1/2 oz. Creme de cacao Italian style syrup
    1/2 oz. Caramel
    1 shot Espresso
            Steamed milk of choice.

Blend. Top with whipped cream.

Creme de Cacao & Coconut Latté

In a 12 oz. cup combine:

    1/2 oz. Creme de cacao Italian style syrup
    1/2 oz. Coconut Italian style syrup
    1 shot Espresso
            Steamed milk of choice.

Blend. Top with whipped cream.

Creme de Cacao & Coffee Latté

In a 12 oz. cup combine:

    1/2 oz. Creme de cacao Italian style syrup
    1/2 oz. Coffee Italian style syrup
    1 shot Espresso
            Steamed milk of choice.

Blend. Top with whipped cream.

Creme de Cacao & Irish Cream Latté

In a 12 oz. cup combine:

    1/2 oz.   Creme de cacao Italian style syrup
    1/2 oz.   Irish cream Italian style syrup
    1 shot   Espresso
             Steamed milk of choice.

Blend. Top with whipped cream.

Creme de Cacao & Orange Latté

In a 12 oz. cup combine:

    1/2 oz.   Creme de cacao Italian style syrup
    1/2 oz.   Orange Italian style syrup
    1 shot   Espresso
             Steamed milk of choice.

Blend. Top with whipped cream.

Creme de Cacao & Raspberry Latté

In a 12 oz. cup combine:

    1/2 oz.   Creme de cacao Italian style syrup
    1/2 oz.   Raspberry Italian style syrup
    1 shot   Espresso
             Steamed milk of choice.

Blend. Top with whipped cream.

Creme de Cacao & Vanilla Latté

In a 12 oz. cup combine:

    1/2 oz.   Creme de cacao Italian style syrup
    1/2 oz.   Vanilla Italian style syrup
    1 shot   Espresso
             Steamed milk of choice.

Blend. Top with whipped cream.

Creme de Menthe Latté

In a 12 oz. cup combine:

    3/4 oz.   Creme de Menthe Italian style syrup
    1 shot   Espresso
             Steamed milk of choice.

Blend. Top with whipped cream.

Creme de Menthe & Vanilla Latté

In a 12 oz. cup combine:

1/2 oz.	Creme de menthe Italian style syrup
1/2 oz.	Vanilla Italian style syrup
1 shot	Espresso
	Steamed milk of choice.

Blend. Top with whipped cream.

Egg Nog Latté

In a 12 oz. cup combine:

1 shot	Espresso
	Steamed Egg Nog.

Blend. Top with whipped cream, and dust lightly with nutmeg.

Ginger Latté

In a 12 oz. cup combine:

1 oz.	Ginger Italian style syrup
1 shot	Espresso
	Steamed milk of choice.

Blend. Top with whipped cream.

Grape Latté

In a 12 oz. cup combine:

1 oz.	Grape Italian style syrup
1 shot	Espresso
	Steamed milk of choice.

Blend. Top with whipped cream.

Grape & Coconut Latté

In a 12 oz. cup combine:

1/2 oz.	Grape Italian style syrup
1/2 oz.	Coconut Italian style syrup
1 shot	Espresso
	Steamed milk of choice.

Blend. Top with whipped cream.

Grape Nut Latté

In a 12 oz. cup combine:

3/4 oz.	Grape Italian style syrup
1/4 oz.	Almond Italian style syrup
1 shot	Espresso
	Steamed milk of choice.

Blend. Top with whipped cream.

Grape & Vanilla Latté

In a 12 oz. cup combine:

1/2 oz.	Grape Italian style syrup
1/2 oz.	Vanilla Italian style syrup
1 shot	Espresso
	Steamed milk of choice.

Blend. Top with whipped cream.

Hazelnut Latté

In a 12 oz. cup combine:

1 oz.	Hazelnut Italian style syrup
1 shot	Espresso
	Steamed milk of choice.

Blend. Top with whipped cream.

Honey Latté

In a 12 oz. cup combine:

1/2 oz.	Honey
1 shot	Espresso
	Steamed milk of choice.

Blend. Top with whipped cream, and dust with cinnamon.

Irish Cream Latté

In a 12 oz. cup combine:

1 oz.	Irish cream Italian style syrup
1 shot	Espresso
	Steamed milk of choice.

Blend. Top with whipped cream.

Irish Cream & Coconut Latté

In a 12 oz. cup combine:

- 1/2 oz. Irish cream Italian style syrup
- 1/2 oz. Coconut Italian style syrup
- 1 shot Espresso
  Steamed milk of choice.

Blend. Top with whipped cream.

Irish Cream & Coffee Latté

In a 12 oz. cup combine:

- 1/2 oz. Irish cream Italian style syrup
- 1/2 oz. Coffee Italian style syrup
- 1 shot Espresso
  Steamed milk of choice.

Blend. Top with whipped cream.

Irish Cream & Creme de Cacao Latté

In a 12 oz. cup combine:

- 1/2 oz. Irish cream Italian style syrup
- 1/2 oz. Creme de cacao Italian style syrup
- 1 shot Espresso
  Steamed milk of choice.

Blend. Top with whipped cream, and garnish with chocolate sprinkles.

Irish Nut Latté

In a 12 oz. cup combine:

- 2/3 oz. Irish cream Italian style syrup
- 1/3 oz. Hazelnut Italian style syrup
- 1 shot Espresso
  Steamed milk of choice.

Blend. Top with whipped cream.

Irish Cream & Orange Latté

In a 12 oz. cup combine:

- 1/2 oz. Irish cream Italian style syrup
- 1/2 oz. Orange Italian style syrup
- 1 shot Espresso
  Steamed milk of choice.

Blend. Top with whipped cream, and drizzle lightly with the orange syrup.

Irish Cream & Vanilla Latté
· ·

In a 12 oz. cup combine:

    1/2 oz. Irish cream Italian style syrup
    1/2 oz. Vanilla Italian style syrup
    1 shot Espresso
            Steamed milk of choice.

Blend. Top with whipped cream.

Latté
· ·

In a 12 oz. cup combine:

    1 shot Espresso
            Steamed milk of choice.

Top with thick velvet foam.

Macadamia Nut Latté
· ·

In a 12 oz. cup combine:

    1 oz.   Macadamia nut Italian style syrup
    1 shot Espresso
            Steamed milk of choice.

Blend. Top with whipped cream.

Macadamia & Coconut Latté
· ·

In a 12 oz. cup combine:

    1/2 oz. Macadamia nut Italian style syrup
    1/2 oz. Coconut Italian style syrup
    1 shot Espresso
            Steamed milk of choice.

Blend. Top with whipped cream.

Mango Latté
· ·

In a 12 oz. cup combine:

    1 oz.   Mango Italian style syrup
    1 shot Espresso
            Steamed milk of choice.

Blend. Top with whipped cream, and garnish with chopped dried mango pieces.

Mango & Almond Latté

In a 12 oz. cup combine:

    3/4 oz. Mango Italian style syrup
    1/4 oz. Almond Italian style syrup
    1 shot   Espresso
             Steamed milk of choice.

Blend. Top with thick velvet foam, and dust lightly with powdered almond.

Mango & Peach Latté

In a 12 oz. cup combine:

    1/2 oz. Mango Italian style syrup
    1/2 oz. Peach Italian style syrup
    1 shot   Espresso
             Steamed milk of choice.

Blend. Top with amaretto or plain whipped cream.

Mango & Vanilla Latté

In a 12 oz. cup combine:

    1/2 oz. Mango Italian style syrup
    1/2 oz. Vanilla Italian style syrup
    1 shot   Espresso
             Steamed milk of choice.

Blend. Top with thick velvet foam, and dust with powdered almond.

Maple Latté

In a 12 oz cup combine:

    3/4 oz. Pure maple syrup
    1 shot   Espresso
             Steamed milk of choice.

Blend. Top with whipped cream.

Monte Cristo Latté

In a 12 oz. cup combine:

    1 oz.   Monte Cristo Italian style syrup
    1 shot   Espresso
             Steamed milk of choice.

Blend. Top with whipped cream.

Orange Latté

In a 12 oz. cup combine:

    1 oz.   Orange Italian style syrup
    1 shot   Espresso
             Steamed milk of choice.

Blend. Top with thick velvet foam, lightly fold the foam in with the Latté.

Orange Nut Latté

In a 12 oz. cup combine:

    3/4 oz. Orange Italian style syrup
    1/4 oz. Hazelnut Italian style syrup
    1 shot   Espresso
             Steamed milk of choice.

Blend. Top with whipped cream, and dust with cinnamon.

Orange & Almond Latté

In a 12 oz. cup combine:

    3/4 oz. Orange Italian style syrup
    1/4 oz. Almond Italian style syrup
    1 shot   Espresso
             Steamed milk of choice.

Blend. Top with whipped cream, and dust lightly with powdered almond.

Orange & Vanilla Latté

In a 12 oz. cup combine:

    1/2 oz. Orange Italian style syrup
    1/2 oz. Vanilla Italian style syrup
    1 shot   Espresso
             Steamed milk of choice.

Blend. Top with thick velvet foam, and dust with powdered vanilla.

Passion Fruit Latté

In a 12 oz. cup combine:

    1 oz.   Passion fruit Italian style syrup
    1 shot   Espresso
             Steamed milk of choice.

Blend. Top with whipped cream, dust lightly with cinnamon.

Passion Fruit & Coffee Latté

In a 12 oz. cup combine:

    1/2 oz.   Passion fruit Italian style syrup
    1/2 oz.   Coffee Italian style syrup
    1 shot   Espresso
              Steamed milk of choice.

Blend. Top with whipped cream.

Passion Fruit & Vanilla Latté

In a 12 oz. cup combine:

    1/2 oz.   Passion fruit Italian style syrup
    1/2 oz.   Vanilla Italian style syrup
    1 shot   Espresso
              Steamed milk of choice.

Blend. Top with whipped cream.

Peanut Butter & Banana Latté

In a 12 oz. cup combine:

    1 oz.   Peanut butter
    1/2 oz.   Banana Italian style syrup
    1 shot   Espresso
              Steamed milk of choice.

Blend. Top with whipped cream.

Peanut Butter & Honey Latté

In a 12 oz. cup combine:

    1 oz.   Peanut butter
    1/3 oz.   Honey (vary to taste)
    1 shot   Espresso
              Steamed milk of choice.

Blend. Top with whipped cream.

Peanut Butter & Jelly Sandwich Latté

In a 12 oz. cup combine:

    1/2 oz.   Peanut butter
    3/4 oz.   Strawberry Italian style syrup*
    1 shot   Espresso
              Steamed milk of choice.

*Can be substituted with raspberry, cherry or grape.

Blend. Top with whipped cream, and drizzle lightly with the strawberry syrup.

Peanut Butter Latté

In a 12 oz. cup combine:

    1 oz.   Peanut butter
    1 shot Espresso
             Steamed milk of choice.

Blend. Top with whipped cream.

Praline Latté

In a 12 oz. cup combine:

    1 oz.   Praline Italian style syrup
    1 shot Espresso
             Steamed milk of choice.

Blend. Top with whipped cream.

Praline & Coffee Latté

In a 12 oz. cup combine:

    1/2 oz. Praline Italian style syrup
    1/2 oz. Coffee Italian style syrup
    1 shot Espresso
             Steamed milk of choice.

Blend. Top with whipped cream.

Raspberry Latté

In a 12 oz. cup combine:

    1 oz.   Raspberry Italian style syrup
    1 shot Espresso
             Steamed milk of choice.

Blend. Top with whipped cream, and drizzle with the raspberry syrup.

Raspberry & Almond Latté

In a 12 oz. cup combine:

    3/4 oz. Raspberry Italian style syrup
    1/4 oz. Almond Italian style syrup
    1 shot Espresso
             Steamed milk of choice.

Blend. Top with whipped cream, and dust lightly with powdered almond.

Raspberry & Banana Latté

In a 12 oz. cup combine:

      3/4 oz. Raspberry Italian style syrup
      1/4 oz. Banana Italian style syrup
      1 shot Espresso
             Steamed milk of choice.

Blend. Top with whipped cream.

Raspberry & Coconut Latté

In a 12 oz. cup combine:

      1/2 oz. Raspberry Italian style syrup
      1/2 oz. Coconut Italian style syrup
      1 shot Espresso
             Steamed milk of choice.

Blend. Top with whipped cream.

Raspberry & Vanilla Latté

In a 12 oz. cup combine:

      1/2 oz. Raspberry Italian style syrup
      1/2 oz. Vanilla Italian style syrup
      1 shot Espresso
             Steamed milk of choice.

Blend. Top with whipped cream.

Rum Latté

In a 12 oz. cup combine:

      1 oz. Rum Italian style syrup
      1 shot Espresso
             Steamed milk of choice.

Blend. Top with whipped cream.

Strawberry Latté

In a 12 oz. cup combine:

      1 oz. Strawberry Italian style syrup
      1 shot Espresso
             Steamed milk of choice.

Blend. Top with whipped cream.

Strawberry & Apple Latté

In a 12 oz. cup combine:

- 1/2 oz.   Strawberry Italian style syrup
- 1/2 oz.   Apple Italian style syrup
- 1 shot   Espresso
- Steamed milk of choice.

Blend. Top whipped cream, dust lightly with cinnamon.

Strawberry & Banana Latté

In a 12 oz. cup combine:

- 1/2 oz.   Strawberry Italian style syrup
- 1/2 oz.   Banana Italian style syrup
- 1 shot   Espresso
- Steamed milk of choice.

Blend. Top with whipped cream.

Strawberry & Vanilla Latté

In a 12 oz. cup combine:

- 1/2 oz.   Strawberry Italian style syrup
- 1/2 oz.   Vanilla Italian style syrup
- 1 shot   Espresso
- Steamed milk of choice.

Blend. Top with whipped cream.

Tamarindo Latté

In a 12 oz. cup combine:

- 1 oz.   Tamarindo Italian style syrup
- 1 shot   Espresso
- Steamed milk of choice.

Blend. Top with whipped cream, and dust lightly with cinnamon.

Vanilla Latté

In a 12 oz. cup combine:

- 1 oz.   Vanilla Italian style syrup
- 1 shot   Espresso
- Steamed milk of choice.

Blend. Top with whipped cream, and dust with powdered vanilla.

Vanilla Fudge Latté

In a 12 oz. cup combine:

1/2 oz.	Vanilla Italian style syrup
1/2 oz.	Chocolate fudge Italian style syrup
1 shot	Espresso
	Steamed milk of choice.

Blend. Top with chocolate flavored whipped cream.

Vanilla Mint Latté

In a 12 oz. cup combine:

3/4 oz.	Vanilla Italian style syrup
1/4 oz.	Creme de menthe Italian style syrup
1 shot	Espresso
	Steamed milk of choice.

Blend. Top with whipped cream, and garnish with a sprig of mint.

Vanilla Nut Latté

In a 12 oz. cup combine:

3/4 oz.	Vanilla Italian style syrup
1/4 oz.	Hazelnut Italian style syrup
1 shot	Espresso
	Steamed milk of choice.

Blend. Top with whipped cream.

Vanilla Peppermint Latté

In a 12 oz. cup combine:

1/2 oz.	Vanilla Italian style syrup
1/2 oz.	Peppermint Italian style syrup
1 shot	Espresso
	Steamed milk of choice.

Blend. Top with whipped cream.

Walnut Latté

In a 12 oz. cup combine:

1 oz.	Walnut Italian style syrup
1 shot	Espresso
	Steamed milk of choice.

Blend. Top with whipped cream.

NICE 'N' SPICY & A BIT OF HONEY

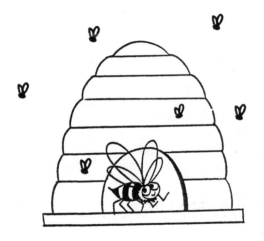

Blueberries & Apple Spice Latté

In a 12 oz. cup combine:

    1/2 oz.   Blueberry Italian style syrup
    1/4 oz.   Cinnamon Italian style syrup
    1/4 oz.   Apple Italian style syrup
    1 shot   Espresso
             Steamed milk of choice.

Blend. Top with whipped cream.

Blueberries & Spice Latté

In a 12 oz. cup combine:

    1/2 oz.   Blueberry Italian style syrup
    1/2 oz.   Cinnamon Italian style syrup
    1 shot   Espresso
             Steamed milk of choice.

Blend. Top with whipped cream, and dust with cinnamon.

Boysenberry & Spice Latté

In a 12 oz. cup combine:

    1/2 oz.   Boysenberry Italian style syrup
    1/2 oz.   Cinnamon Italian style syrup
    1 shot   Espresso
             Steamed milk of choice.

Blend. Top with whipped cream, and dust with cinnamon.

Cherries & Spice Latté

In a 12 oz. cup combine:

    1/2 oz.   Cherry Italian style syrup
    1/2 oz.   Cinnamon Italian style syrup
    1 shot   Espresso
             Steamed milk of choice.

Blend. Top with whipped cream, and dust with cinnamon.

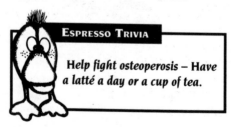

ESPRESSO TRIVIA

Help fight osteoperosis – Have a latté a day or a cup of tea.

Cinnamon & Sugar Latté

In a 12 oz. cup combine:

3/4 oz. Cinnamon Italian style syrup
1 pkg.   Sugar*
1 shot   Espresso
         Steamed milk of choice.

*May be substituted with artificial sweetner.

Blend. Top with whipped cream, and garnish with cinnamon-brown sugar granules.

Honey Butter Latté

In a 12 oz. cup combine:

2 tsp.   Honey butter
1 shot   Espresso
         Steamed milk of choice.

Blend. Top with whipped cream.

Honey Butter Nut Latté

In a 12 oz. cup combine:

1 tsp.   Honey butter
1/2 oz. Hazelnut Italian style syrup
1 shot   Espresso
         Steamed milk of choice.

Blend. Top with whipped cream.

Honey Butter & Cinnamon Latté

In a 12 oz. cup combine:

1 tsp.   Honey butter
1/2 oz. Cinnamon Italian style syrup
1 shot   Espresso
         Steamed milk of choice.

Blend. Top with whipped cream, and dust with cinnamon.

Honey Butter & Peach Latté

In a 12 oz. cup combine:

1 tsp.   Honey butter
1/2 oz. Peach Italian style syrup
1 shot   Espresso
         Steamed milk of choice.

Blend. Top with whipped cream.

Ginger 'n' Cinnamon Spice Latté

In a 12 oz. cup combine:

- 1/2 oz.   Ginger Italian style syrup
- 1/2 oz.   Cinnamon Italian style syrup
- 1 shot   Espresso
    Steamed milk of choice.

Blend. Top with whipped cream, and sprinkle with cinnamon-brown sugar granules.

Ginger 'n' Orange Spice Latté

In a 12 oz. cup combine:

- 1/3 oz.   Ginger Italian style syrup
- 1/3 oz.   Orange Italian style syrup
- 1/3 oz.   Cinnamon Italian style syrup
- 1 shot   Espresso
    Steamed milk of choice.

Blend. Top with whipped cream, and garnish with cinnamon-brown sugar granules.

Honey Nut Latté (Nuttin' Honey)

In a 12 oz. cup combine:

- 1 tsp.   Honey
- 1/2 oz.   Hazelnut Italian style syrup
- 1 shot   Espresso
    Steamed milk of choice.

Blend. Top with whipped cream.

Orange & Cinnamon Spice Latté

In a 12 oz. cup combine:

- 1/2 oz.   Orange Italian style syrup
- 1/2 oz.   Cinnamon Italian style syrup
- 1 shot   Espresso
    Steamed milk of choice.

Blend. Top with whipped cream, and dust lightly with cinnamon.

Peach Cobbler Latté

In a 12 oz. cup combine:

- 1 tsp.   Honey butter
- 1/3 oz.   Peach Italian style syrup
- 1/3 oz.   Cinnamon Italian style syrup
- 1 shot   Espresso
    Steamed milk of choice.

Blend. Top with whipped cream, and dust with nutmeg-brown sugar granules.

Peaches & Spice Latté ....

In a 12 oz. cup combine:

1/2 oz.   Peach Italian style syrup
1/2 oz.   Cinnamon Italian style syrup
1 shot   Espresso
         Steamed milk of choice.

Blend. Top with whipped cream, and dust with cinnamon.

Raspberries & Spice Latté ....

In a 12 oz. cup combine:

1/2 oz.   Raspberry Italian style syrup
1/2 oz.   Cinnamon Italian style syrup
1 shot   Espresso
         Steamed milk of choice.

Blend. Top with whipped cream, and dust with cinnamon.

ESPRESSO TRIVIA

In Prague, cappuccinos have foam, but are topped with whipped cream.

Italians sweeten their espresso with sugar.

French have their espresso with equal parts of milk.

Austrians top their espresso with whipped cream.

Some places in the United States a cappuccino is made the same as a latté!

= Cherry Latté

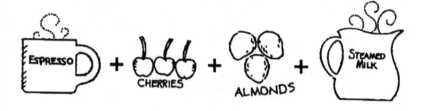

= Cherry Nut Latté

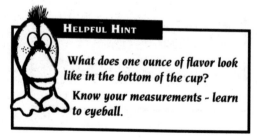

HELPFUL HINT

What does one ounce of flavor look like in the bottom of the cup?

Know your measurements - learn to eyeball.

Happy Hour To The Rescue

Amaretto Latté
. . . .

In a 12 oz. cup combine:

    1 oz.   Amaretto Italian style syrup
    1 shot Espresso
             Steamed milk of choice.

Blend. Top with amaretto flavored whipped cream.

Amaretto 'n' Coffee Latté
. . . .

In a 12 oz. cup combine:

    1/2 oz. Amaretto Italian style syrup
    1/2 oz. Coffee Italian style syrup
    1 shot Espresso
             Steamed milk of choice.

Blend. Top with amaretto flavored whipped cream.

Apricot Brandy Latté
. . . .

In a 12 oz. cup combine:

    1/2 oz. Apricot Italian style syrup
    1/2 oz. Amaretto Italian style syrup
    1 shot Espresso
             Steamed milk of choice.

Blend. Top with whipped cream.

B 52 Latté
. . . .

In a 12 oz. cup combine:

    1 oz.   B 52 Italian style syrup
    1 shot Espresso
             Steamed milk of choice.

Blend. Top with whipped cream.

ESPRESSO TRIVIA

What two words are most often heard at an espresso cart?
I *need.*

Blackberry Wine Latté

In a 12 oz. cup combine:

3/4 oz.	Blackberry Italian style syrup
1/4 oz.	Amaretto Italian style syrup
1 shot	Espresso
	Steamed milk of choice.

Blend. Top with whipped cream

Boysenberry Wine Latté

In a 12 oz. cup combine:

3/4 oz.	Boysenberry Italian style syrup
1/4 oz.	Amaretto Italian style syrup
1 shot	Espresso
	Steamed milk of choice.

Blend. Top with whipped cream.

Brandied Cherries Latté

In a 12 oz. cup combine:

2/3 oz.	Wild cherry Italian style syrup
1/3 oz.	Amaretto Italian style syrup
1 shot	Espresso
	Steamed milk of choice.

Blend. Top with whipped cream.

Café Mexico

In a 12 oz. cup combine:

1/2 oz.	Café Mexico Italian style syrup
1/4 oz.	Vanilla Italian style syrup
1/4 oz.	Almond Italian style syrup
1 shot	Espresso
	Steamed milk of choice.

Blend. Top with whipped cream.

Creme de Menthe & Amaretto Latté

In a 12 oz. cup combine:

1/2 oz.	Creme de menthe Italian style syrup
1/2 oz.	Amaretto Italian style syrup
1 shot	Espresso
	Steamed milk of choice.

Blend. Top with whipped cream.

Egg Nog McDaniels Latté

In a 12 oz. cup combine:

1/3 oz.	Amaretto Italian style syrup
1 shot	Espresso
	Steamed eggnog.

Blend. Top with whipped cream, dust with nutmeg. **Better than the real thing!**

Grape Wine Latté

In a 12 oz. cup combine:

3/4 oz.	Grape Italian style syrup
1/4 oz.	Amaretto Italian style syrup
1 shot	Espresso
	Steamed milk of choice.

Blend. Top with whipped cream.

Irish Cream Latté

In a 12 oz. cup combine:

1 oz.	Irish cream Italian style syrup
1 shot	Espresso
	Steamed milk of choice.

Blend. Top with whipped cream.

Irish Cream & Amaretto Latté

In a 12 oz. cup combine:

1/2 oz.	Irish cream Italian style syrup
1/2 oz.	Amaretto Italian style syrup
1 shot	Espresso
	Steamed milk of choice.

Blend. Top with whipped cream.

ESPRESSO TRIVIA

What's poetic justice?
That first sip of your early morning latté.

Irish Java Latté

In a 12 oz. cup combine:
- 1/2 oz.   Irish cream Italian style syrup
- 1/2 oz.   Coffee Italian style syrup
- 1 shot   Espresso
- Steamed milk of choice.

Blend. Top with whipped cream.

Java Jumble Latté

In a 12 oz. cup combine:
- 1/3 oz.   Amaretto Italian style syrup
- 1/3 oz.   Irish cream Italian style syrup
- 1/3 oz.   Coffee Italian style syrup
- 1 shot   Espresso
- Steamed milk of choice.

Blend. Top with whipped cream.

Kahlua Cream Latté

In a 12 oz. cup combine:
- 1 oz.   Coffee Italian style syrup
- 1 shot   Espresso
- Steamed milk of choice.

Blend. Top with whipped cream.

Kahlua Rumba Latté

In a 12 oz. cup combine:
- 1/2 oz.   Coffee Italian style syrup
- 1/2 oz.   Rum Italian style syrup
- 1 shot   Espresso
- Steamed milk of choice.

Blend. Top with whipped cream.

Mexican Rumba Latté

In a 12 oz. cup combine:
- 2/3 oz.   Café Mexico Italian style syrup
- 1/3 oz.   Rum Italian style syrup
- 1 shot   Espresso
- Steamed milk of choice.

Blend. Top with plain or amaretto flavored whipped cream.

Orange Brandy Latté

In a 12 oz. cup combine:

2/3 oz.   Orange Italian style syrup*
1/3 oz.   Amaretto Italian style syrup*
1 shot   Espresso
Steamed milk of choice.

*Or use 1 oz. Orange Brandy Italian style syrup as substitute for both of these.

Blend. Top with whipped cream.

Peach Schnapps Latté

In a 12 oz. cup combine:

3/4 oz.   Peach Italian style syrup
1/4 oz.   Amaretto Italian style syrup
1 shot   Espresso
Steamed milk of choice.

Blend. Top with whipped cream. **Try this one on ice!**

Raspberry Brandy Latté

In a 12 oz. cup combine:

3/4 oz.   Raspberry Italian style syrup
1/4 oz.   Amaretto Italian style syrup
1 shot   Espresso
Steamed milk of choice.

Blend. Top with whipped cream.

Rum Heaven Latté

In a 12 oz. cup combine:

1/2 oz.   Rum Italian style syrup
1/2 oz.   Amaretto Italian style syrup
1 shot   Espresso
Steamed milk of choice.

Blend. Top with whipped cream.

Strawberry Brandy Latté

In a 12 oz. cup combine:

3/4 oz.   Strawberry Italian style syrup
1/4 oz.   Amaretto Italian style syrup
1 shot   Espresso
Steamed milk of choice.

Blend. Top with whipped cream.

Spanish Coffee Latté . . . .

In a 12 oz. cup combine:

    1 oz.   Spanish coffee Italian style syrup
    1 shot   Espresso
           Steamed milk of choice.

Blend. Top with foamed milk.

Spanish & Coffee Latté . . . .

In a 12 oz. cup combine:

    1/2 oz.   Spanish coffee Italian style syrup
    1/2 oz.   Coffee Italian style syrup
    1 shot   Espresso
            Steamed milk of choice.

Blend. Top with whipped cream.

Spanish Coffee Rum Latté . . . .

In a 12 oz. cup combine:

    1/2 oz.   Spanish Coffee Italian style syrup
    1/2 oz.   Rum Italian style syrup
    1 shot   Espresso
            Steamed milk of choice.

Blend. Top with amaretto flavored whipped cream.

ESPRESSO TRIVIA

What's the difference between a tall and a grande?

The espresso cart you are at.

The espresso bar is the bar of the 90's.

Where does everyone know your name?

   A. *Boston*
   B. *Church*
   C. *Espresso Bar*

Three major coffee producing regions are the Americas, Africa and Indonesia.

Brazil is the world's largest coffee producer.

Coffee plants take up to five years to mature and produce fruit.

Many of the coffee characteristics are determined by soil, climate, weather conditions, elevation and region in which it has been grown.

Coffee sacks are usually made from the tough strong fibers of the hemp plant. This herb plants unique leaves are used for hashish/marijuana.

Home espresso machines are becoming very popular. They even have ones you can take camping!

Daring? Try scrambling a few eggs with your steam wand.

What the heck is orgeat? Almond Italian style syrup.

What's an espresso wardrobe? Someone not good at juggling lattés.

CUP OF HEAVEN

Brevé

- Thick Velvet Foam from the steamed Half & Half
- Steamed Half & Half
- Espresso

12 oz. cup

Flavored Brevé

- Whipped Cream & Garnish
- Steamed Half & Half
- Espresso
- Flavor

12 oz. cup

Apple Waldorf Brevé

In a 12 oz. cup combine:

1/2 oz.	Apple Italian style syrup
1/4 oz.	Hazelnut Italian style syrup
1/4 oz.	Cinnamon Italian style syrup
1 shot	Espresso
	Steamed Half and Half.

Blend. Top with whipped cream, and garnish with nutmeg-brown sugar granules.

Bavarian Chocolate Latté

In a 12 oz. cup combine:

1 oz.	Bavarian chocolate Italian style syrup
1 shot	Espresso
	Steamed milk of choice.

Blend. Top with whipped cream, and sprinkle with chocolate-brown sugar granules.

Bavarian Mint Latté

In a 12 oz. cup combine:

1/2 oz.	Coffee Italian style syrup
1/2 oz.	Chocolate mint Italian style syrup
1 shot	Espresso
	Steamed milk of choice.

Blend. Top with whipped cream.

Belgian Waffle Brevé

In a 12 oz. cup combine:

1/2 oz.	Vanilla Italian style syrup
1/4 oz.	Walnut Italian style syrup
1/4 oz.	Pure maple syrup
1 shot	Espresso
	Steamed Half and Half.

Blend. Top with whipped cream, drizzle with strawberry Italian style syrup, and garnish with a strawberry slice.

Black Walnut Latté

In a 12 oz. cup combine:

3/4 oz.	Macadamia nut Italian style syrup*
1/4 oz.	Hazelnut Italian style syrup*
1 shot	Espresso
	Steamed milk of choice.

Or use Walnut Italian style syrup as a substitute for both of these.

Blend. Top with whipped cream, dust with cinnamon.

Blueberries 'n' Cream Brevé

In a 12 oz. cup combine:

3/4 oz.	Blueberry Italian style syrup*
1/4 oz.	Vanilla Italian style syrup
1 shot	Espresso
	Steamed Half and Half.

Can be substituted with cherry, raspberry, boysenberry or orange.

Blend. Top with whipped cream.

Butter Nut Latté

In a 12 oz. cup combine:

1/2 oz.	Butterscotch topping
1/2 oz.	Hazelnut Italian style syrup
1 shot	Espresso
	Steamed milk of choice.

Blend. Top with whipped cream.

ESPRESSO TRIVIA

Egg nog and Brevés should be steamed to a lower temperature (about 145°) than the other milks.

Providing a daily special is a great way to encourage your customers to try a new flavor of drink.

Butter Pecan Latté

In a 12 oz. cup combine:

1/2 oz.	Butterscotch topping*
1/4 oz.	Hazelnut Italian style syrup*
1/4 oz.	Almond Italian style syrup*
1 shot	Espresso
	Steamed milk of choice.

Blend. Top with whipped cream.

Butterscotch Latté

In a 12 oz. cup combine:

1 oz.	Butterscotch topping
1 shot	Espresso
	Steamed milk of choice.

Blend. Top with whipped cream.

Butter Coffee Toffee Latté

In a 12 oz. cup combine:

1/2 oz.	Coffee Italian style syrup
1/2 oz.	Butterscotch topping
1 shot	Espresso
	Steamed milk of choice.

Blend. Top with whipped cream.

Butter Toffee Latté

In a 12 oz. cup combine:

1/2 oz.	Vanilla Italian style syrup
1/2 oz.	Butterscotch topping
1 shot	Espresso
	Steamed milk of choice.

Blend. Top with whipped cream.

Caramel Latté

In a 12 oz. cup combine:

1 oz.	Caramel topping
1 shot	Espresso
	Steamed milk of choice.

Blend. Top with whipped cream.

Caramel Nut Latté (Sugar Daddy) . . . .

In a 12 oz. cup combine:
- 1/2 oz.   Caramel topping
- 1/2 oz.   Hazelnut Italian style syrup
- 1 shot   Espresso
- Steamed milk of choice.

Blend. Top with whipped cream.

Cherry Blossom Surprise Brevé . . . .

In a 12 oz. cup combine:
- 1/2 oz.   Cherry Italian style syrup
- 1/2 oz.   Orange Italian style syrup
- 1/4 oz.   Walnut Italian style syrup
- 1 shot   Espresso
- Steamed Half and Half.

Blend. Top with amaretto flavored whipped cream.

Chocolate Macadamia Nut Torte Latté . . . .

In a 12 oz. cup combine:
- 1/2 oz.   Creme de cacao Italian style syrup
- 1/2 oz.   Macadamia nut Italian style syrup
- 1 shot   Espresso
- Steamed milk of choice.

Blend. Top with whipped cream, and drizzle with chocolate syrup. Garnish with a macadamia nut.

Chocolate Peanut Butter Pie Latté . . . .

In a 12 oz. cup combine:
- 1/2 oz.   Peanut butter*
- 3/4 oz.   Chocolate syrup*
- 1 shot   Espresso
- Steamed milk of choice.

*Or use 1 oz. Chocolate peanut butter Italian style syrup as a substitute for both of these.

Blend. Top with whipped cream, and garnish with chocolate sprinkles. Better than a piece of chocolate peanut butter pie!

Chocolate Walnut Torte Latté

In a 12 oz. cup combine:

    1/2 oz.   Creme de cacao Italian style syrup
    1/2 oz.   Walnut Italian style syrup
    1 shot   Espresso
            Steamed milk of choice.

Blend. Top with whipped cream, and drizzle lightly with chocolate syrup and garnish with chopped walnuts.

Cinnamon 'n' Honey Latté   (*Soo very very good!*)

In a 12 oz. cup combine:

    1 tsp.   Honey
    3/4 oz.   Cinnamon Italian style syrup
    1 shot   Espresso
            Steamed milk of choice.

Blend. This drink needs nothing else. It's great!

Cinnamon Roll Latté

In a 12 oz. cup combine:

    1/2 oz.   Cinnamon Italian style syrup
    1 tsp.   Brown sugar (vary to taste)
    1 shot   Espresso
            Steamed milk of choice.

Blend. Top with whipped cream, and a dash of cinnamon.

Cinnamon Nut Roll Latté

In a 12 oz. cup combine:

    1/2 oz.   Cinnamon Italian style syrup
    1/4 oz.   Hazelnut Italian style syrup
    1 tsp.   Brown sugar
    1 shot   Espresso
            Steamed milk of choice.

Blend. Top with whipped cream, and a dash of cinnamon.

Chocolate Pecan Brevé

In a 12 oz. cup combine:

    1/2 oz.   Chocolate syrup
    1/2 oz.   Pecan Italian style syrup
    1 shot   Espresso
            Steamed milk of choice.

Blend. Top with whipped cream, and garnish with chocolate-brown sugar granules.

Coconut Haystack Latté

In a 12 oz. cup combine:

- 1/2 oz. Caramel topping
- 1/2 oz. Coconut Italian style syrup
- 1 shot Espresso
- Steamed milk of choice.

Blend. Top with whipped cream.

Coffee 'n' Orange Cream Brevé

In a 12 oz. cup combine:

- 1/2 oz. Coffee Italian style syrup
- 1/2 oz. Orange Italian style syrup
- 1 shot Espresso
- Steamed Half and Half.

Blend. Top with whipped cream.

Coffee Pecan Brevé

In a 12 oz. cup combine:

- 1/2 oz. Coffee Italian style syrup
- 1/2 oz. Butter pecan Italian style syrup
- 1 shot Espresso
- Steamed Half and Half.

Blend. Top with whipped cream, and garnish with cinnamon-brown sugar granules.

Cookies Cream 'n' Mint Latté

In a 12 oz. cup combine:

- 3/4 oz. Chocolate mint Italian style syrup
- 1/4 oz. Amaretto Italian style syrup
- 1 shot Espresso
- Steamed milk of choice.

Blend. Top with amaretto flavored whipped cream.

Danny's Special Latté

In a 12 oz. cup combine:

- 1 pkge. Artificial sweetner
- 1 shot Espresso
- Steamed milk of choice.

Blend. Top with thick velvet foam, and dust lightly with powdered vanilla.

Egg Nog Latté

In a 12 oz. cup combine:

1 shot Espresso
Steamed Egg Nog.

Blend. Top with a dash of nutmeg. **Hint:** Egg Nog with thicken after steaming, so only steam small amounts or enough for each drink.

English Toffee Mint Latté

In a 12 oz. cup combine:

1/2 oz. Caramel topping
1/4 oz. Coffee Italian style syrup
1/4 oz. Chocolate mint Italian style syrup
1 shot Espresso
Steamed milk of choice.

Blend. Top with whipped cream.

French Vanilla Nut Brevé

In a 12 oz. cup combine:

3/4 oz. Vanilla Italian style syrup
1/4 oz. Hazelnut Italian style syrup
1 shot Espresso
Steamed Half and Half.

Blend. Top with whipped cream.

Gingersnap Latté

In a 12 oz. cup combine:

3/4 oz. Ginger Italian style syrup
1/4 oz. Cinnamon Italian style syrup
1 shot Espresso
Steamed milk of choice.

Blend. Top with whipped cream, and dust lightly with cinnamon.

Granola Bar Latté

In a 12 oz. cup combine:

1/4 oz. Molasses
1/4 oz. Honey
1/2 oz. Coconut Italian style syrup
1 shot Espresso
Steamed milk of choice.

Blend. Top with whipped cream. **Serve with a Granola Bar!**

Hot Scotch Latté

In a 12 oz. cup combine:

1/4 oz.	Butterscotch topping
1/4 oz.	Amaretto Italian style syrup
1/2 oz.	Chocolate syrup
1 shot	Espresso
	Steamed milk of choice.

Blend. Top with amaretto flavored whipped cream.

Irish Mint Latté

In a 12 oz. cup combine:

3/4 oz.	Caramel topping
1/4 oz.	Creme de menthe Italian style syrup
1 shot	Espresso
	Steamed milk of choice.

Blend. Top with whipped cream.

Maple Nut Latté

In a 12 oz. cup combine:

1/2 oz.	Pure maple syrup
1/2 oz.	Walnut Italian style syrup
1 shot	Espresso
	Steamed milk of choice.

Blend. Top with whipped cream.

Marzipan Orange Brevé

In a 12 oz. cup combine:

3/4 oz.	Orange Italian style syrup
1/4 oz.	Amaretto Italian style syrup
1 shot	Espresso
	Steamed Half and Half.

Blend. Top with amaretto flavored whipped cream.

Pralines 'n' Cream Brevé

In a 12 oz. cup combine:

3/4 oz.	Hazelnut Italian style syrup*
1/4 oz.	Almond Italian style syrup*
1 shot	Espresso
	Steamed Half and Half.

*Or use 1 oz. Praline Italian style syrup as a substitue for both of these

Blend. Top with whipped cream, and garnish with cinnamon-brown sugar granules.

Raspberry Walnut Torte Latté
....

In a 12 oz. cup combine:

- 1/2 oz.   Chocolate syrup
- 1/4 oz.   Raspberry Italian style syrup
- 1/4 oz.   Walnut Italian style syrup
- 1 shot   Espresso
  Steamed milk of choice.

Blend. Top with whipped cream, and drizzle with raspberry Italian style syrup.

Snickerdoodle Latté
....

In a 12 oz. cup combine:

- 1 oz.   Vanilla Italian style syrup
- 1 shot   Espresso
  Steamed milk of choice.

Blend. Top with whipped cream, and dust lightly with cinnamon. **Serve with a snickerdoodle cookie. Makes for a great daily special.**

Three Some Latté
....

In a 12 oz. cup combine:

- 1/3 oz.   Coffee Italian style syrup
- 1/3 oz.   Coconut Italian style syrup
- 1/3 oz.   Creme de cacao Italian style syrup
- 1 shot   Espresso
  Steamed milk of choice.

Blend. Top with whipped cream.

Toasted Coconut Cream Brevé
....

In a 12 oz. cup combine:

- 3/4 oz.   Coconut Italian style syrup
- 1/4 oz.   Hazelnut Italian style syrup
- 1 shot   Espresso
  Steamed Half and Half.

Blend. Top with whipped cream.

Toffee Mint Latté
....

In a 12 oz. cup combine:

- 2/3 oz.   Coffee Italian style syrup
- 1/3 oz.   Creme de menthe Italian style syrup
- 1 shot   Espresso
  Steamed milk of choice.

Blend. Top with whipped cream, and garnish with chocolate sprinkles.

ICED LATTÉS

Iced Latté

Ice

Espresso

Cold Milk

Any Latté or Brevé can be iced – these are just a few.

16 oz. cup

Iced Almond Latté
· ·

In a 16 oz. glass combine:

    1 oz.   Almond Italian style syrup
    1 shot Espresso

Add enough cold milk to fill glass about 2/3 full. Fill remainder of glass with ice. Stir.

Iced Amaretto Latté
· ·

In a 16 oz. glass combine:

    1 oz.   Amaretto Italian style syrup
    1 shot Espresso

Add enough cold milk to fill glass about 2/3 full. Fill remainder of glass with ice. Stir.

Iced Caramel Latté
· ·

In a 16 oz. glass combine:

    1 oz.   Caramel topping
    1 shot Espresso
             Blend well.

Add enough cold milk to fill glass about 2/3 full. Fill remainder of glass with ice. Stir.

Iced Chocolate Mint Latté
· ·

In a 16 oz. glass combine:

    1 oz.   Chocolate mint Italian style syrup
    1 shot Espresso

Add enough cold milk to fill glass about 2/3 full. Fill remainder of glass with ice. Stir.

82

Iced Cinnamon Latté · · · · · · · · · · · · · · · · · ·

In a 16 oz. glass combine:

    1 oz.   Cinnamon Italian style syrup
    1 shot Espresso

Add enough cold milk to fill glass about 2/3 full. Fill remainder of glass with ice. Stir.

Iced Cherry Nut Latté · · · · · · · · · · · · · · · · ·

In a 16 oz. glass combine:

    3/4 oz. Cherry Italian style syrup
    1/4 oz. Almond Italian style syrup
    1 shot Espresso

Add enough cold milk to fill glass about 2/3 full. Fill remainder of glass with ice. Stir.

Iced Creme de Cacao Latté · · · · · · · · · · · · ·

In a 16 oz. glass combine:

    1 oz.   Creme de cacao Italian style syrup
    1 shot Espresso

Add enough cold milk to fill glass about 2/3 full. Fill remainder of glass with ice. Stir.

Iced Coffee Latté ·

In a 16 oz. glass combine:

    1 oz.   Coffee Italian style syrup
    1 shot Espresso

Add enough cold milk to fill glass about 2/3 full. Fill remainder of glass with ice. Stir.

Iced Ginger Latté ·

In a 16 oz. glass combine:

    1 oz.   Ginger Italian style syrup
    1 shot Espresso

Add enough cold milk to fill glass about 2/3 full. Fill remainder of glass with ice. Stir.

Iced Hazelnut Latté · · · · · · · · · · · · · · · · · ·

In a 16 oz. glass combine:

    1 oz.   Hazelnut Italian style syrup
    1 shot Espresso

Add enough cold milk to fill glass about 2/3 full. Fill remainder of glass with ice. Stir.

Iced Irish Cream Latté

In a 16 oz. glass combine:

    1 oz.   Irish cream Italian style syrup
    1 shot Espresso

Add enough cold milk to fill glass about 2/3 full. Fill remainder of glass with ice. Stir.

Iced Latté

In a 16 oz. glass combine:

    1 shot Espresso

Add enough cold milk to fill glass about 2/3 full. Fill remainder of glass with ice. Stir.

Iced Maple Nut Latté

In a 16 oz. glass combine:

    3/4 oz. Pure maple syrup
    1/4 oz. Walnut Italian style syrup
    1 shot Espresso

Add enough cold milk to fill glass about 2/3 full. Fill remainder of glass with ice. Stir.

Iced Nutty Orange Latté

In a 16 oz. glass combine:

    3/4 oz. Orange Italian style syrup
    1/4 oz. Almond Italian style syrup
    1 shot Espresso

Add enough cold milk to fill glass about 2/3 full. Fill remainder of glass with ice. Stir.

Iced Raspberry Latté

In a 16 oz. glass combine:

    1 oz.   Raspberry Italian style syrup
    1 shot Espresso

Add enough cold milk to fill glass about 2/3 full. Fill remainder of glass with ice. Stir.

Iced Vanilla Latté

In a 16 oz. glass combine:

    1 oz.   Vanilla Italian style syrup
    1 shot Espresso

Add enough cold milk to fill glass about 2/3 full. Fill remainder of glass with ice. Stir.

MOCHA MADNESS

Mocha

- Whipped Cream & Garnish
- Steamed Milk
- Espresso Chocolate Syrup

12 oz. cup

Flavored Mocha

- Whipped Cream & Garnish
- Steamed Milk
- Espresso
- Chocolate Syrup
- Flavored Syrup

12 oz. cup

Almond Mocha - 1

In a 12 oz. cup combine:

1/2 oz.   Almond Italian style syrup
1/2 oz.   Chocolate syrup
1 shot   Espresso
Steamed milk of choice.

Blend. Top with whipped cream, and dust with powdered almond.

Almond Mocha - 2

In a 12 oz. cup combine:

1/4 oz.   Almond Italian style syrup
3/4 oz.   Chocolate syrup
1 shot   Espresso
Steamed milk of choice.

Blend. Top with whipped cream, and dust with powdered almond.

Almond Mocha Joy

In a 12 oz. cup combine:

1/4 oz.   Coconut Italian style syrup
1/4 oz.   Almond Italian style syrup
1/2 oz.   Chocolate syrup
1 shot   Espresso
Steamed milk of choice.

Blend. Top with whipped cream, garnish with toasted coconut.

Almond Mocha Roca

In a 12 oz. cup combine:

1/2 oz.	Butterscotch topping
1/4 oz.	Almond Italian style syrup
1/2 oz.	Chocolate syrup
1 shot	Espresso
	Steamed milk of choice.

Blend. Top with whipped cream, garnish with a mini candy bar.

Amaretto Mocha

In a 12 oz. cup combine:

1/3 oz.	Amaretto Italian style syrup
3/4 oz.	Chocolate syrup
1 shot	Espresso
	Steamed milk of choice.

Blend. Top with amaretto flavored whipped cream.

Amaretto Nut Mocha

In a 12 oz. cup combine:

1/4 oz.	Amaretto Italian style syrup
1/4 oz.	Hazelnut Italian style syrup
1/2 oz.	Chocolate syrup
1 shot	Espresso
	Steamed milk of choice.

Blend. Top with whipped cream.

Banana Nut Mocha

In a 12 oz. cup combine:

1/2 oz.	Banana Italian style syrup
1/4 oz.	Hazelnut Italian style syrup
1/2 oz.	Chocolate syrup
1 shot	Espresso
	Steamed milk of choice.

Blend. Top with whipped cream, top with a banana chip.

Basic Mocha

In a 12 oz. cup combine:

1 oz.	Chocolate syrup
1 shot	Espresso
	Steamed milk of choice.

Blend. Top with whipped cream.

Blackberry Mocha

In a 12 oz. cup combine:

      1/2 oz.   Blackberry Italian style syrup
      1/2 oz.   Chocolate syrup
      1 shot   Espresso
               Steamed milk of choice.

Blend. Top with whipped cream, drizzle with the blackberry syrup.

Black Cherry Mocha

In a 12 oz. cup combine:

      1/2 oz.   Black cherry Italian style syrup
      1/2 oz.   Chocolate syrup
      1 shot   Espresso
               Steamed milk of choice.

Blend. Top with whipped cream.

Butter Pecan Mocha

In a 12 oz. cup combine:

      1/2 oz.   Butter pecan Italian style syrup
      1/2 oz.   Chocolate syrup
      1 shot   Espresso
               Steamed milk of choice.

Blend. Top with whipped cream.

Butterscotch Mocha

In a 12 oz. cup combine:

      1/2 oz.   Butterscotch topping
      1/2 oz.   Chocolate syrup
      1 shot   Espresso
               Steamed milk of choice.

Blend. Top with whipped cream.

Caramel Mocha

In a 12 oz. cup combine:

      1/2 oz.   Caramel topping
      1/2 oz.   Chocolate syrup
      1 shot   Espresso
               Steamed milk of choice.

Blend. Top with whipped cream.

Caramel Nut Mocha

In a 12 oz. cup combine:
- 1/2 oz.   Caramel topping
- 1/4 oz.   Hazelnut Italian style syrup
- 3/4 oz.   Chocolate syrup
- 1 shot   Espresso
  Steamed milk of choice.

Blend. Top with whipped cream.

Cherry Coconut Mocha

In a 12 oz. cup combine:
- 1/4 oz.   Cherry Italian style syrup
- 1/4 oz.   Coconut Italian style syrup
- 1/2 oz.   Chocolate syrup
- 1 shot   Espresso
  Steamed milk of choice.

Blend. Top with whipped cream.

Cherry Mocha

In a 12 oz. cup combine:
- 1/2 oz.   Cherry Italian style syrup
- 1/2 oz.   Chocolate syrup
- 1 shot   Espresso
  Steamed milk of choice.

Blend. Top with whipped cream.

Cherry Nut Mocha

In a 12 oz. cup combine:
- 1/4 oz.   Cherry Italian style syrup
- 1/4 oz.   Almond Italian style syrup
- 1/2 oz.   Chocolate syrup
- 1 shot   Espresso
  Steamed milk of choice.

Blend. Top with whipped cream.

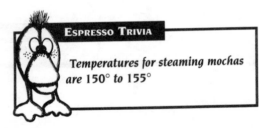

ESPRESSO TRIVIA

Temperatures for steaming mochas are 150° to 155°

Chocolate Covered Cherry Mocha

In a 12 oz. cup combine:

    1/2 oz.   Cherry Italian style syrup
    1/2 oz.   Chocolate syrup
    1 shot   Espresso
              Steamed milk of choice.

Blend. Top with whipped cream.

Cinnamon Mocha

In a 12 oz. cup combine:

    1/2 oz.   Cinnamon Italian style syrup
    1/2 oz.   Chocolate syrup
    1 shot   Espresso
              Steamed milk of choice.

Blend. Top with whipped cream.

Coconut Mocha

In a 12 oz. cup combine:

    1/2 oz.   Coconut Italian style syrup
    1/2 oz.   Chocolate syrup
    1 shot   Espresso
              Steamed milk of choice.

Blend. Top with whipped cream.

Coconut Nut Mocha

In a 12 oz. cup combine:

    1/4 oz.   Coconut Italian style syrup
    1/4 oz.   Hazelnut Italian style syrup
    1/2 oz.   Chocolate syrup
    1 shot   Espresso
              Steamed milk of choice.

Blend. Top with whipped cream.

Coffee Mint Mocha

In a 12 oz. cup combine:

    1/2 oz.   Coffee Italian style syrup
    1/4 oz.   Creme de menthe Italian style syrup
    1/2 oz.   Chocolate syrup
    1 shot   Espresso
              Steamed milk of choice.

Blend. Top with whipped cream.

Coffee Mocha . . . .

In a 12 oz. cup combine:

1/2 oz.	Coffee Italian style syrup
1/2 oz.	Chocolate syrup
1 shot	Espresso
	Steamed milk of choice.

Blend. Top with whipped cream.

Coffee Nut Mocha . . . .

In a 12 oz. cup combine:

1/2 oz.	Coffee Italian style syrup
1/4 oz.	Hazelnut Italian style syrup
1/2 oz.	Chocolate syrup
1 shot	Espresso
	Steamed milk of choice.

Blend. Top with whipped cream.

Creme de Cacao & Coconut Mocha . . . .

In a 12 oz. cup combine:

1/4 oz.	Creme de cacao Italian style syrup
1/4 oz.	Coconut Italian syle syrup
1/2 oz.	Chocolate syrup
1 shot	Espresso
	Steamed milk of choice.

Blend. Top with whipped cream.

Creme de Cacao Mocha . . . .

In a 12 oz. cup combine:

1/2 oz.	Creme de cacao Italian style syrup
1/2 oz.	Chocolate syrup
1 shot	Espresso
	Steamed milk of choice.

Blend. Top with whipped cream, garnish with grated chocolate.

Egg Nog Mocha . . . .

In a 12 oz. cup combine:

1 oz.	Bittersweet chocolate syrup
1 shot	Espresso
	Steamed Egg Nog.

Blend. Top with whipped cream. **Chocolate cheese cake in a cup!**

French Vanilla Nut Mocha

In a 12 oz. cup combine:

1/4 oz.	Vanilla Italian style syrup
1/4 oz.	Hazelnut Italian style syrup
1/2 oz.	Chocolate syrup
1 shot	Espressso
	Steamed milk of choice.

Blend. Top with whipped cream, dust with cinnamon.

German Chocolate Mocha

In a 12 oz. cup combine:

1/4 oz.	Caramel topping
1/4 oz.	Coconut Italian style syrup
1/4 oz.	Hazelnut Italian style syrup
1/2 oz.	Chocolate syrup
1 shot	Espresso
	Steamed milk of choice.

Blend. Top with whipped cream, Garnish with toasted coconut.

German Chocolate Peanut Butter Pie Mocha

In a 12 oz. cup combine:

1/2 oz.	Peanut butter*
1/4 oz.	Coconut Italian style syrup
1/4 oz.	Caramel topping
1/2 oz.	Chocolate syrup*
1 shot	Espresso
	Steamed milk of choice.

*Or use 3/4 oz. chocolate peanut butter Italian style syrup as a subtitute for both of these.

Blend. Top with whipped cream, and garnish with chocolate sprinkles.

Hazelnut Mocha

In a 12 oz. cup combine:

1/3	Hazelnut Italian style syrup
3/4	Chocolate syrup
1 shot	Espresso
	Steamed milk of choice.

Blend. Top with whipped cream.

Irish Cream Mocha

In a 12 oz. cup combine:

        1/2 oz.   Irish cream Italian style syrup
        1/2 oz.   Chocolate syrup
        1 shot   Espresso
                   Steamed milk of choice.

Blend. Top with whipped cream.

Irish Mint Mocha

In a 12 oz. cup combine:

        1/2 oz.   Caramel topping
        1/4 oz.   Creme de menthe Italian style syrup
        1/2 oz.   Chocolate syrup
        1 shot   Espresso
                   Steamed milk of choice.

Blend. Top with whipped cream, garnish with a piece of mint candy.

Irish Nut Mocha

In a 12 oz. cup combine:

        1/2 oz.   Irish cream Italian style syrup
        1/4 oz.   Hazelnut Italian style syrup
        1/2 oz.   Chocolate syrup
        1 shot   Espresso
                   Steamed milk of choice.

Blend. Top with whipped cream.

Kahlua Mocha Mousse

In a 12 oz. cup combine:

        1/2 oz.   Coffee Italian style syrup
        1/2 oz.   Chocolate syrup
        1 shot   Espresso
                   Steamed milk of choice.

Blend. Top with whipped cream, garnish with grated bitter chocolate.

Macadamia Nut Mocha

In a 12 oz. cup combine:

        1/2 oz.   Macadamia Italian style syrup
        1/2 oz.   Chocolate syrup
        1 shot   Espresso
                   Steamed milk of choice.

Blend. Top with whipped cream, garnish with a macadamia nut.

Mango Mocha

In a 12 oz. cup combine:

1/2 oz.	Mango Italian style syrup
1/2 oz.	Chocolate syrup
1 shot	Espresso.
	Steamed milk of choice.

Blend. Top with *amaretto flavored whipped cream.*

Mango Nut Mocha

In a 12 oz. cup combine:

1/4 oz.	Mango Italian style syrup
1/4 oz.	Hazelnut Italian style syrup
1/2 oz.	Chocolate syrup
1 shot	Espresso
	Steamed milk of choice.

Blend. Top with *whipped cream.*

Maple Bar Mocha

In a 12 oz. cup combine:

1/2 oz.	Pure maple syrup
1/2 oz.	Chocolate syrup
1 shot	Espresso
	Steamed milk of choice.

Blend. Top with *whipped cream.*

Maple Nut Mocha

In a 12 oz. cup combine:

1/2 oz.	Chocolate Italian style syrup
1/2 oz.	Pure maple syrup
1/4 oz.	Hazelnut Italian style syrup
1 shot	Espresso
	Steamed milk of choice.

Blend. Top with *whipped cream.*

Mexican Mocha

In a 12 oz. cup combine:

1 oz.	Mexican powdered chocolate
1 shot	Espresso
	Steamed milk of choice.

Blend. Top with *whipped cream.*

Mocha Lite

In a 12 oz. cup combine:

1 pack	Sugar free powdered cocoa
1 shot	Espresso
	Non-fat steamed milk.

Blend. Top with foam.

Mocha Malt

In a 12 oz. cup combine:

3 tsp.	Powdered Malt flavor*
1 oz.	Chocolate syrup*
1 shot	Espresso
	Steamed milk of choice.

*Or use 1 oz. chocolate malt Italian style syrup as a substitute for both of these.

Blend. Top with whipped cream.

Mocha Mint

In a 12 oz. cup combine:

1/4 oz.	Creme de menthe Italian style syrup
3/4 oz.	Chocolate syrup
1 shot	Espresso
	Steamed milk of choice.

Blend. Top with whipped cream.

Mocha Tamarindo

In a 12 oz. cup combine:

1/2 oz.	Tamarindo Italian style syrup
1/2 oz.	Chocolate syrup
1 shot	Espresso
	Steamed milk of choice.

Blend. Top with whipped cream.

Orange Nut Mocha

In a 12 oz. cup combine:

1/4 oz.	Orange Italian style syrup
1/4 oz.	Hazelnut Italian style syrup
1/2 oz.	Chocolate syrup
1 shot	Espresso
	Steamed milk of choice.

Blend. Top with whipped cream.

Mocha Rumba
In a 12 oz. cup combine:
- 1/2 oz.   Rum Italian style syrup
- 1/2 oz.   Chocolate syrup
- 1 shot   Espresso
-          Steamed milk of choice.

Blend. Top with whipped cream.

Orange Slice Mocha
In a 12 oz. cup combine:
- 1/2 oz.   Orange Italian style syrup
- 1/2 oz.   Chocolate syrup
- 1 shot   Espresso
-          Steamed milk of choice.

Blend. Top with whipped cream.

Raspberry Mocha
In a 12 oz. cup combine:
- 1/2 oz.   Raspberry Italian style syrup
- 1/2 oz.   Chocolate syrup
- 1 shot   Espresso
-          Steamed milk of choice.

Blend. Top with whipped cream.

Raspberry Nut Mocha
In a 12 oz. cup combine:
- 1/4 oz.   Raspberry Italian style syrup
- 1/4 oz.   Almond Italian style syrup
- 1/2 oz.   Chocolate syrup
- 1 shot   Espresso
-          Steamed milk of choice.

Blend. Top with whipped cream.

Rocky Road Mocha
In a 12 oz. cup combine:
- 1/4 oz.   Hazelnut Italian style syrup
- 1 oz.   Chocolate syrup
- 1 shot   Espresso
-          Steamed milk of choice.

Blend. Top with mini-marshmallows or marshmallow creme.

Strawberry Coconut Mocha

In a 12 oz. cup combine:

    1/4 oz. Strawberry Italian style syrup
    1/4 oz. Coconut Italian style syrup
    1/2 oz. Chocolate syrup
    1 shot Espresso
            Steamed milk of choice.

Blend. Top with whipped cream.

Strawberry Mocha

In a 12 oz. cup combine:

    1/2 oz. Strawberry Italian style syrup
    1/2 oz. Chocolate syrup
    1 shot Espresso
            Steamed milk of choice.

Blend. Top with whipped cream.

Strawberry Mocha Malt

In a 12 oz. cup combine:

    3 tsp. Powdered Malt flavor*
    1/2 oz. Strawberry Italian style syrup
    1/2 oz. Chocolate syrup*
    1 shot Espresso
            Steamed milk of choice.

> *Or use 1 oz. chocolate malt Italian style syrup as a substitute for both of these.

Blend. Top with whipped cream. **Serve this one to grandma!**

Vanilla Mocha

In a 12 oz. cup combine:

    1/2 oz. Vanilla Italian style syrup
    1/2 oz. Chocolate syrup
    1 shot Espresso
            Steamed milk of choice.

Blend. Top with whipped cream.

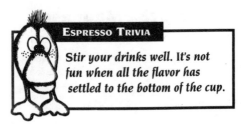

ESPRESSO TRIVIA

Stir your drinks well. It's not fun when all the flavor has settled to the bottom of the cup.

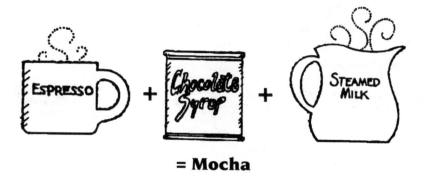

= **Mocha**

= **Almond Mocha**

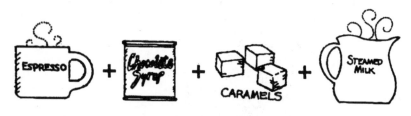

= **Mocha Madness**

ICED MOCHAS

Iced Mocha

- Whipped Cream & Garnish
- Ice
- Cold Milk
- Espresso
- Chocolate Syrup

16 oz. glass (cold cup)

Iced Flavored Mocha

- Whipped Cream & Garnish
- Ice
- Cold Milk
- Espresso
- Chocolate Syrup
- Flavored Syrup

16 oz. glass (cold cup)

Iced Almond Mocha

In a 16 oz. glass combine:

    1 oz.   Chocolate syrup
    1/4 oz. Almond Italian style syrup
    1 shot Espresso

Blend well. Add enough cold milk to fill glass about 2/3 full. Fill remainder of glass with ice.

Iced Banana Mocha

In a 16 oz. glass combine:

    3/4 oz. Chocolate syrup
    1/2 oz. Banana Italian style syrup
    1 shot Espresso

Blend well. Add enough cold milk to fill glass about 2/3 full. Fill remainder of glass with ice.

Iced Banana Nut Mocha

In a 16 oz. glass combine:

    3/4 oz. Chocolate syrup
    1/4 oz. Hazelnut Italian style syrup
    1/4 oz. Banana Italian style syrup
    1 shot Espresso

Blend well. Add enough cold milk to fill glass about 2/3 full. Fill remainder of glass with ice.

Iced Blackberry Mocha

In a 16 oz. glass combine:

    3/4 oz. Chocolate syrup
    1/2 oz. Blackberry Italian style syrup
    1 shot Espresso

Blend well. Add enough cold milk to fill glass about 2/3 full. Fill remainder of glass with ice.

Iced Caramel Mocha

In a 16 oz. glass combine:

    1/2 oz. Chocolate syrup
    1/2 oz. Caramel topping
    1 shot Espresso

Blend well. Add enough cold milk to fill glass about 2/3 full. Fill remainder of glass with ice.

Iced Chocolate Covered Cherries Mocha

In a 16 oz. glass combine:

  3/4 oz.   Chocolate syrup
  1/2 oz.   Cherry Italian style syrup
  1 shot   Espresso

Blend well. Add enough cold milk to fill glass about 2/3 full. Fill remainder of glass with ice.

Iced Cinnamon Mocha

In a 16 oz. glass combine:

  3/4 oz.   Chocolate syrup
  1/2 oz.   Cinnamon Italian style syrup
  1 shot   Espresso

Blend well. Add enough cold milk to fill glass about 2/3 full. Fill remainder of glass with ice.

Iced Coconut Mocha

In a 16 oz. glass combine:

  3/4 oz.   Chocolate syrup
  1/2 oz.   Coconut Italian style syrup
  1 shot   Espresso

Blend well. Add enough cold milk to fill glass about 2/3 full. Fill remainder of glass with ice.

Iced Coffee Mocha

In a 16 oz. glass combine:

  3/4 oz.   Chocolate syrup
  1/2 oz.   Coffee Italian style syrup
  1 shot   Espresso

Blend well. Add enough cold milk to fill glass about 2/3 full. Fill remainder of glass with ice.

Iced Irish Nut Mocha

In a 16 oz. glass combine:

  1/2 oz.   Chocolate syrup
  1/2 oz.   Irish cream Italian style syrup
  1/4 oz.   Hazelnut Italian style syrup
  1 shot   Espresso

Blend well. Add enough cold milk to fill glass about 2/3 full. Fill remainder of glass with ice.

Iced Hazelnut Mocha

In a 16 oz. glass combine:

      3/4 oz.   Chocolate syrup
      1/2 oz.   Hazelnut Italian style syrup
      1 shot   Espresso

Blend well. Add enough cold milk to fill glass about 2/3 full. Fill remainder of glass with ice.

Iced Maple Nut Mocha

In a 16 oz. glass combine:

      1/2 oz.   Chocolate syrup
      1/2 oz.   Pure Maple syrup
      1/4 oz.   Hazelnut Italian style syrup

Blend well.Add enough cold milk to fill glass about 2/3 full. Fill remainder of glass with ice.

Iced Mocha

In a 16 oz. glass combine:

      1 oz.   Chocolate syrup
      1 shot   Espresso

Blend well. Add enough cold milk to fill glass about 2/3 full. Fill remainder of glass with ice.

Iced Mocha Mint

In a 16 oz. glass combine:

      1 oz.   Chocolate syrup
      1/4 oz.   Creme de menthe Italian style syrup
      1 shot   Espresso

Blend well. Add enough cold milk to fill glass about 2/3 full. Fill remainder of glass with ice.

Iced Praline Mocha

In a 16 oz. glass combine:

      3/4 oz.   Chocolate syrup
      1/2 oz.   Praline Italian style syrup

Blend well. Add enough cold milk to fill glass about 2/3 full. Fill remainder of glass with ice.

Iced Orange Mocha

In a 16 oz. glass combine:

    1/2 oz.   Chocolate syrup
    1/2 oz.   Orange Italian style syrup

Blend well. Add enough cold milk to fill glass about 2/3 full. Fill remainder of glass with ice.

Iced Raspberry Mocha

In a 16 oz. glass combine:

    3/4 oz.   Chocolate syrup
    1/2 oz.   Raspberry Italian style syrup
    1 shot   Espresso

Blend well. Add enough cold milk to fill glass about 2/3 full. Fill remainder of glass with ice.

Iced Rum Mocha

In a 16 oz. glass combine:

    3/4 oz.   Chocolate syrup
    1/2 oz.   Rum Italian style syrup
    1 shot   Espresso

Blend well. Add enough cold milk to fill glass about 2/3 full. Fill remainder of glass with ice.

Iced Vanilla Mocha

In a 16 oz. glass combine:

    3/4 oz.   Chocolate syrup
    1/2 oz.   Vanilla Italian style syrup
    1 shot   Espresso

Blend well. Add enough cold milk to fill glass about 2/3 full. Fill remainder of glass with ice.

ESPRESSO TRIVIA

Be sure to dissolve the heavy flavors with a warm shot of espresso - then add the cold milk and blend.

HOLIDAY SPECIALS

NEW YEAR'S DAY

Double Grande Mocha

In a 16 oz. cup combine:

      1 1/4 oz. Chocolate Syrup

    2 shots Espresso

             Steamed milk of choice

Blend. Top with whipped cream.

For the resolution...

Non-fat Latté

In a 12 oz. cup combine:

    1 shot   Espresso

           Steamed non-fat milk.

Top with thick velvet-like foam.

Chocolate Covered Cherry Mocha

In a 12 oz. cup combine:

1/2 oz.	Cherry Italian style syrup
1/2 oz.	Chocolate syrup
1 shot	Espresso
	Steamed milk of choice

Blend. Top with whipped cream and a maraschino cherry.

Dark Chocolate Nut Espresso Truffle

In a 8 oz. cup combine:

1/2 oz.	Bittersweet chocolate
1/4 oz.	Walnut Italian style syrup
1 shot	Espresso

Blend well. Let cool for 1 minute. Fill cup 3/4 full with whipped cream. Whip together until thick and fluffy. Top with whipped cream, and dust with chocolate powder.

PRESIDENT'S DAY

TALK ABOUT A LATTE ON THE ROCKS!

Cherry Pie Ala Mode Latté

In a 12 oz. cup combine:

1 oz.	Cherry Italian style syrup
1 shot	Espresso
	Steamed milk of choice

Blend. Top with whipped cream and a dash of cinnamon.

Cherry Nut Italian Soda

In a 16 oz. glass (cold cup) combine:

2 oz.	Cherry Italian style syrup
1/2 oz.	Almond Italian style syrup
Ice	To fill glass 3/4 full

Fill remainder of glass with club soda. Blend. Top with whipped cream.

Amalfis: Add 1 oz. of Half and Half. (float on top)
Cremosa: Blend in 1 oz. of Half and Half.

Irish Mint Latté . . . .

In a 12 oz. cup combine:

3/4 oz.	Caramel topping
1/4 oz.	Creme de menthe Italian style syrup
1 shot	Espresso
	Steamed milk of choice

Blend. Top with whipped cream and mint sprinkles.

Irish Cream Latté . . . .

In a 12 oz. cup combine:

1 oz.	Irish cream Italian style syrup
1 shot	Espresso
	Steamed milk of choice

Blend. Top with whipped cream.

EASTER

Grape Wine Latté

In a 12 oz. cup combine:

3/4 oz.	Grape Italian style syrup
1/4 oz.	Amaretto Italian style syrup
1 shot	Espresso
	Steamed milk of choice

Blend. Top with whipped cream and jelly beans. Serve with hot cross buns!

Jelly Bean Italian Soda

In a 16 oz. glass (cold cup) combine:

1 oz.	Stawberry Italian style syrup
1 oz.	Licorice Italian style syrup
Ice	To fill glass 3/4 full

Fill remainder of glass with club soda. Blend. Top with whipped cream.

Amalfis: Add 1 oz. of Half and Half. (float on top)
Cremosa: Blend in 1 oz. of Half and Half.

Snickerdoodle Latté
. . . .

In a 12 oz. cup combine:

   1 oz.   Vanilla Italian style syrup
   1 shot   Espresso
            Steamed milk of choice

Blend. Top with whipped cream and a dash of cinnamon. Serve with Snickerdoodle cookies.

Praline Silk
. . . .

In a 12 oz. cup combine:

   1/2 oz.   Praline Italian style syrup
   3/4 oz.   White chocolate
   1 shot   Espresso
             Steamed milk of choice

Blend. Top with whipped cream.

Apple Pie Ala Mode Latté

In a 12 oz. cup combine:

1 oz.	Apple Italian style syrup
1 shot	Espresso
	Steamed milk of choice

Blend. Top with whipped cream. Dust with nutmeg.

Strawberry Cream Italian Soda

In a 16 oz. glass (cold cup) combine:

1 oz.	Stawberry Italian style syrup
1 oz.	Vanilla Italian style syrup
Ice	To fill glass 3/4 full

Fill remainder of glass with club soda. Blend. Top with whipped cream.

    Amalfis: Add 1 oz. of Half and Half. *(float on top)*
    Cremosa: Blend in 1 oz. of Half and Half.

FATHER'S DAY

Mocha Malt

In a 12 oz. cup combine:

3 tsp.	Powdered malt flavor
1 oz.	Chocolate syrup
1 shot	Espresso
	Steamed milk of choice

Blend. Top with whipped cream and chocolate sprinkles.

Black Cherry Italian Soda

In a 16 oz. glass (cold cup) combine:

2 oz.	Black cherry Italian style syrup
Ice	To fill glass 3/4 full

Fill remainder of glass with club soda. Blend. Top with whipped cream.

Amalfis: Add 1 oz. of Half and Half. (float on top)
Cremosa: Blend in 1 oz. of Half and Half.

113

INDEPENDENCE DAY

Iced Mocha Mint Julip

In a 16 oz. glass (cold cup) combine:

1 oz.	Chocolate syrup
1/4 oz.	Creme de menthe Italian style syrup
1 shot	Espresso

Blend well. Add enough cold milk to fill the glass about 2/3 full. Fill remainder of the glass with ice. Topped with whipped cream.

Watermelon Italian Soda

In a 16 oz. glass (cold cup) combine:

2 oz.	Watermelon Italian style syrup
Ice	To fill glass 3/4 full

Fill remainder of glass with club soda. Blend. Top with whipped cream.

Amalfis: Add 1 oz. of Half and Half. (float on top)
Cremosa: Blend in 1 oz. of Half and Half.

LABOR DAY

Iced Raspberry Mocha

In a 16 oz. glass (cold cup) combine:

- 1/2 oz.   Raspberry Italian style syrup
- 1 oz.   Chocolate syrup
- 1 shot   Espresso

Blend well. Add enough cold milk to fill the glass about 2/3 full. Fill remainder of the glass with ice. Topped with whipped cream.

Irish Cream Italian Soda

In a 16 oz. glass (cold cup) combine:

- 2 oz.   Irish Cream Italian style syrup
- Ice   To fill glass 3/4 full

Fill remainder of glass with club soda. Blend. Top with whipped cream.

Amalfis: Add 1 oz. of Half and Half. (float on top)
Cremosa: Blend in 1 oz. of Half and Half.

Double Tall Latté

· ·

In a 12 oz. cup combine:

    2 shots Espresso
             Steamed milk of choice

Top with thick velvet-like foam.

Ginger Italian Soda

· ·

In a 16 oz. glass (cold cup) combine:

    2 oz.   Ginger Italian style syrup
    Ice   To fill glass 3/4 full

Fill remainder of glass with club soda. Blend. Top with whipped cream.

      Amalfis: *Add 1 oz. of Half and Half. (float on top)*
      Cremosa: *Blend in 1 oz. of Half and Half.*

Carameled Apple Latté

In a 12 oz. cup combine:

1/2 oz.	Apple Italian style syrup
3/4 oz.	Caramel topping
1 shot	Espresso
	Steamed milk of choice

Blend. Top with whipped cream.

Warlocks Potion

In a fresh "Hot" shot of espresso brew one bag of Licorice Herbal Tea. Let steep while steaming the milk.

In a 12 oz. cup combine:

1/2 oz.	Licorice Italian style syrup
	Shot of espresso (tea bag removed)
	Steamed milk of choice

Blend. Top with whipped cream and garnish with licorice candy.

THANKSGIVING

Egg Nog Latté

In a 12 oz. cup combine:

    1 shot   Espresso
              Steamed Egg Nog

Top with whipped cream and a dash of nutmeg.

Cranberry Italian Soda

In a 16 oz. glass (cold cup) combine:

    2 oz.   Cranberry Italian style syrup
    Ice   To fill glass 3/4 full

Fill remainder of glass with club soda. Blend. Top with whipped cream.

    Amalfis: Add 1 oz. of Half and Half. (float on top)
    Cremosa: Blend in 1 oz. of Half and Half.

Candy Cane Latté
· ·

In a 12 oz. cup combine:

      3/4 oz. Cherry Italian style syrup
      1/4 oz. Creme de menthe Italian style syrup
      1 shot   Espresso
                Steamed milk of choice

Blend. Top with whipped cream and serve with small candy canes.

Marzipan Orange Brevé
· ·

In a 12 oz. cup combine:

      3/4 oz. Orange Italian style syrup
      1/4 oz. Amaretto Italian style syrup
      1 shot   Espresso
                Steamed Half and Half

Blend. Top with whipped cream.

THE CHOICE IS YOURS!

THIS YEAR YOU CAN DRINK N' DRIVE—THE CHOICE IS YOURS!

Egg Nog McDaniels

In a 12 oz. cup combine:

1/3 oz.	Amaretto Italian style syrup
1 shot	Espresso
	Steamed Egg Nog

Blend. Top with whipped cream and a dash of nutmeg.

Mexican Rumba Latté

In a 12 oz. cup combine:

2/3 oz.	Cafe Mexico Italian style syrup
1/3 oz.	Rum Italian style syrup
1 shot	Espresso
	Steamed milk of choice

Blend. Top with whipped cream.

WHITE CHOCOLATE

WHITE CHOCOLATE BASIC RECIPE

In the microwave or doubleboiler, slowly melt one 12oz. package (2cups) of white vanilla chips with 3/4 cup milk, stirring constantly until smooth and all the chips are melted. If using the microwave, melt the chips at 50 second intervals, stirring at each interval. Refrigerate in an airtight container, keeps about 10 days. Use a one ounce ice cream scoop to measure portions needed.

Recommended portions based on cup size:

8oz. cup - 3/4 oz. white chocolate base
12oz. cup - 1-1/4 oz. white chocolate base
16oz. cup - 1-1/2 oz. white chocolate base

WHITE CHOCOLATE POWDER

The white chocolate powder can be used as it comes, in the recommended portions.

Recommended portions based on cup size:

8 oz. cup 3 tablespoons white chocolate powder
12 oz. cup 4 tablespoons white chocolate powder
16 oz. cup 5 tablespoons white chocolate powder

When making a white chocolate drink, use portions equivalent to the type of white chocolate that you chose to use.

Double Boiler

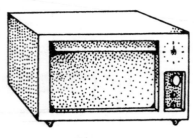

Microwave

Caramel Silk Latté

In a 12 oz. cup combine:

1/2 oz.	Caramel topping
3/4 oz.	White chocolate
1 shot	Espresso
	Steamed milk of choice.

Blend. Top with whipped cream.

Coconut Macadamia Nut Latté

In a 12 oz. cup combine:

1/3 oz.	Coconut Italian style syrup
1/3 oz.	Macadamia nut Italian style syrup
2/3 oz.	White chocolate
1 shot	Espresso
	Steamed milk of choice.

Blend. Top with whipped cream. Garnish with toasted coconut & a macadamia nut.

Coconut Macaroon Latté

In a 12 oz. cup combine:

3/4 oz.	White chocolate
1/2 oz.	Coconut Italian style syrup
1/4 oz.	Almond Italian style syrup
1 shot	Espresso
	Steamed milk of choice.

Blend. Top with whipped cream and garnish with toasted coconut.

Honey Nougat Latté

In a 12 oz. cup combine:

1/2 oz.	Honey
3/4 oz.	White chocolate
1 shot	Espresso
	Steamed milk of choice.

Blend. Top with thick velvet foam. Drizzle lightly with Walnut Italian style syrup.

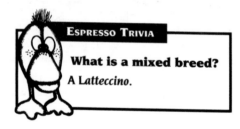

ESPRESSO TRIVIA

What is a mixed breed?

A *Latteccino.*

Maple Nougat Latté . . . .

In a 12 oz. cup combine:

1/2 oz.	Pure maple syrup
3/4 oz	White chocolate
1 shot	Espresso
	Sreamed milk of choice.

Blend. Top with whipped cream, drizzle lightly with the maple syrup.

Walnut Nougat Latté . . . .

In a 12 oz. cup combine:

1/2 oz.	Walnut Italian style syrup
3/4 oz.	White chocolate
1 shot	Espresso
	Steamed milk of choice.

Blend. Top with whipped cream. Garnish with a walnut half.

Praline Silk Latté . . . .

In a 12 oz. cup combine:

1/2 oz.	Praline Italian style syrup
3/4 oz	White chocolate
1 shot	Espresso
	Steamed milk of choice.

Blend. Top with whipped cream. Garnish with cinnamon brown sugar granules.

Raspberry Nougat Latté . . . .

In a 12 oz. cup combine:

1/2 oz.	Raspberry Italian style syrup
3/4 oz	White chocolate
1 shot	Espresso
	Steamed milk of choice.

Blend. Top with whipped cream, drizzle lightly with the raspberry syrup.

White Chocolate Latté . . . .

In a 12 oz. cup combine:

1-1/4 oz	White chocolate
1 shot	Espresso
	Steamed milk of choice.

Blend. Top with whipped cream. Garnish with a white chocolate covered espresso bean.

White Milk Chocolate Latté

In a 12 oz. cup combine:

1/2 oz.	Chocolate syrup
3/4 oz.	White chocolate
1 shot	Espresso
	Sreamed milk of choice.

Blend. Top with whipped cream. Garnish with chocolate sprinkles.

White Chocolate Creme de Menthe

In a 12 oz. cup combine:

1/2 oz.	Creme de menthe Italian style syrup
1/2 oz.	White chocolate
1 shot	Espresso
	Steamed milk of choice.

Blend. Top with whipped cream, drizzle lightly with the creme de menthe syrup.

Vanilla Nut Nougat Latté

In a 12 oz. cup combine:

1/2 oz.	Vanilla Italian style syrup
1/4 oz	Walnut Italian style syrup
1/2 oz.	White chocolate
1 shot	Espresso
	Steamed milk of choice.

Blend. Top with whipped cream, drizzle lightly with the walnut syrup.

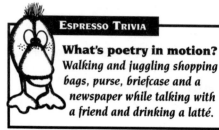

ESPRESSO TRIVIA

What's poetry in motion?
Walking and juggling shopping bags, purse, briefcase and a newspaper while talking with a friend and drinking a latté.

STEAMERS

Non-Espresso Drinks

Yes, the whole family can enjoy a drink at the espresso bar! Any one of the flavored lattes or mochas can be made into a great tasting "non-coffee" drink just by omitting the espresso. Mom and Dad can have their lattes and mochas, and the kids can enjoy a flavored steamed milk.

Steamers

Foam or
Whipped Topping

Steamed Milk
135° - 145°

Flavored Syrup

12 oz. cup

FLAVORED MOO STEAMERS
BASE RECIPE

In a 12 oz. cup combine:

  1 oz. Italian style syrup flavor of choice
         Frothed / Steamed milk of choice

Blend. Top with whipped cream or thick velvet foam. Garnish.

Some suggested flavored moo steamers

Almond Moo Steamer
Banana Moo Steamer
Blackberry Moo Steamer
Butter Pecan Moo Steamer
Caramel Moo Steamer
Cherry Moo Steamer
Chocolate Moo Steamer (*same as hot chocolate*)
Chocolate Mint Moo Steamer
Creme de Menthe Moo Steamer
Coconut Moo Steamer
Egg Nog Moo Steamer (*just steamed egg nog*)
Kiwi Moo Steamer
Raspberry Moo Steamer
Strawberry Moo Steamer
Watermelon Moo Steamer

ITALIAN SODAS

VARIATIONS FOR ITALIAN SODAS

Amalfis: An Italian soda with the Half and Half floated on top.

Cremosa: An Italian soda blended with Half and Half.

Italian Cream Soda: Made the same way as a cremosa.

Italian Smoothie: A version of the Italian cream soda, that has been crushed in a blender.

Italian Soda: Club soda flavored with an Italian style syrup, combined with ice.

BASIC ITALIAN SODA RECIPE

In a 16 oz. glass (cold cup) add:

2 1/2 oz.   Syrup flavor of choice
Ice To fill glass 3/4 full

Fill glass with club soda or seltzer water. Leave room if adding Half and Half. Blend. Top with whipped cream.

****Syrups differ in taste, at times you may need to adjust the amount according to the brand.****

ITALIAN SODA TRIVIA

Sugar free and non-fat Italian style syrups mix and blend as well as the regular syrups.

Italian Soda

Garnish — Whipped Topping

Club Soda/Ice

Flavored Syrup

16 oz. glass (cold cup)

Almond Italian Soda

In a 16 oz. glass (cold cup) add:

2 oz.	Almond Italian style syrup
Ice	To fill glass 3/4 full

Fill remainder of glass with club soda. Blend. Top with whipped cream.

Amalfis: Add 1 oz. of Half and Half. (float on top)
Cremosa: Blend in 1 oz. of Half and Half.

Amaretto Italian Soda

In a 16 oz. glass (cold cup) add:

2 oz.	Amaretto Italian style syrup
Ice	To fill glass 3/4 full

Fill remainder of glass with club soda. Blend. Top with whipped cream.

Amalfis: Add 1 oz. of Half and Half. (float on top)
Cremosa: Blend in 1 oz. of Half and Half.

Apple Cinnamon Italian Soda

In a 16 oz. glass (cold cup) add:

1 oz.	Apple Italian style syrup
1 oz.	Cinnamon Italian style syrup
Ice	To fill glass 3/4 full

Fill remainder of glass with club soda. Blend. Top with whipped cream.

Amalfis: Add 1 oz. of Half and Half. (float on top)
Cremosa: Blend in 1 oz. of Half and Half.

Apricot Almond Italian Soda

In a 16 oz. glass (cold cup) add:

1 1/2 oz.	Apricot Italian style syrup
1/2 oz.	Almond Italian style syrup
Ice	To fill glass 3/4 full

Fill remainder of glass with club soda. Blend. Top with whipped cream.

Amalfis: Add 1 oz. of Half and Half. (float on top)
Cremosa: Blend in 1 oz. of Half and Half.

Banana Cream Pie Italian Soda

In a 16 oz. glass (cold cup) add:

2 oz.	Banana Italian style syrup
Ice	To fill glass 3/4 full

Fill remainder of glass with club soda. Blend. Top with whipped cream.

Amalfis: Add 1 oz. of Half and Half. (float on top)
Cremosa: Blend in 1 oz. of Half and Half.

Banana Melon Italian Soda

In a 16 oz. glass (cold cup) add:

1 oz.	Banana Italian style syrup
1 oz.	Melon Italian style syrup
Ice	To fill glass 3/4 full

Fill remainder of glass with club soda. Blend. Top with whipped cream.

Amalfis: Add 1 oz. of Half and Half. (float on top)
Cremosa: Blend in 1 oz. of Half and Half.

Blackberry Italian Soda

In a 16 oz. glass (cold cup) add:

2 oz.	Blackberry Italian style syrup
1/2 oz.	Banana Italian style syrup
Ice	To fill glass 3/4 full

Fill remainder of glass with club soda. Blend. Top with whipped cream.

Amalfis: Add 1 oz. of Half and Half. (float on top)
Cremosa: Blend in 1 oz. of Half and Half.

Black Cherry Italian Soda

In a 16 oz. glass (cold cup) add:

2 oz.	Black cherry Italian style syrup
Ice	To fill glass 3/4 full

Fill remainder of glass with club soda. Blend. Top with whipped cream.

Amalfis: Add 1 oz. of Half and Half. (float on top)
Cremosa: Blend in 1 oz. of Half and Half.

Black Cherry Nut Italian Soda

In a 16 oz. glass (cold cup) add:

2 oz.	Black cherry Italian style syrup
1/4 oz.	Almond Italian style syrup
Ice	To fill glass 3/4 full

Fill remainder of glass with club soda. Blend. Top with whipped cream.

Amalfis: Add 1 oz. of Half and Half. (float on top)
Cremosa: Blend in 1 oz. of Half and Half.

Blueberry Italian Soda

In a 16 oz. glass (cold cup) add:

2 1/2 oz.	Blueberry Italian style syrup
Ice	To fill glass 3/4 full

Fill remainder of glass with club soda. Blend. Top with whipped cream.

Amalfis: Add 1 oz. of Half and Half. (float on top)
Cremosa: Blend in 1 oz. of Half and Half.

Boysenberry & Vanilla Italian Soda

In a 16 oz. glass (cold cup) add:

1 1/2 oz.	Boysenberry Italian style syrup
1 oz.	Vanilla Italian style syrup
Ice	To fill glass 3/4 full

Fill remainder of glass with club soda. Blend. Top with whipped cream.

Amalfis: Add 1 oz. of Half and Half. (float on top)
Cremosa: Blend in 1 oz. of Half and Half.

Bubble Gum Italian Soda

In a 16 oz. glass (cold cup) add:

1 oz.	Strawberry Italian style syrup
1 oz.	Cherry Italian style syrup
1/2 oz.	Blueberry Italian style syrup
Ice	To fill glass 3/4 full

Fill remainder of glass with club soda. Blend. Top with whipped cream.

Amalfis: Add 1 oz. of Half and Half. (float on top)
Cremosa: Blend in 1 oz. of Half and Half.

Cherry Italian Soda

In a 16 oz. glass (cold cup) add:

2 oz.	Cherry Italian style syrup
Ice	To fill glass 3/4 full

Fill remainder of glass with club soda. Blend. Top with whipped cream.

Amalfis: Add 1 oz. of Half and Half. (float on top)
Cremosa: Blend in 1 oz. of Half and Half.

Cherry Coconut Italian Soda

In a 16 oz. glass (cold cup) add:

2 oz.	Cherry Italian style syrup
1/2 oz.	Coconut Italian style syrup
Ice	To fill glass 3/4 full

Fill remainder of glass with club soda. Blend. Top with whipped cream.

Amalfis: Add 1 oz. of Half and Half. (float on top)
Cremosa: Blend in 1 oz. of Half and Half.

Cherry Cola Italian Soda

In a 16 oz. glass (cold cup) add:

1 oz.	Cola Italian style syrup
1 oz.	Cherry Italian style syrup
Ice	To fill glass 3/4 full

Fill remainder of glass with club soda. Blend. Top with whipped cream.

Amalfis: Add 1 oz. of Half and Half. (float on top)
Cremosa: Blend in 1 oz. of Half and Half.

Cherry Nut Italian Soda

In a 16 oz. glass (cold cup) add:

2 oz.	Cherry Italian style syrup
1/2 oz.	Almond Italian style syrup
Ice	To fill glass 3/4 full

Fill remainder of glass with club soda. Blend. Top with whipped cream.

Amalfis: Add 1 oz. of Half and Half. (float on top)
Cremosa: Blend in 1 oz. of Half and Half.

Cherry Sour Cream Pie Italian Soda

In a 16 oz. glass (cold cup) add:

2 oz.	Cherry Italian style syrup
1/2 oz.	Lemon Italian style syrup
Ice	To fill glass 3/4 full

Fill remainder of glass with club soda. Blend. Top with whipped cream.

Amalfis: Add 1 oz. of Half and Half. (float on top)
Cremosa: Blend in 1 oz. of Half and Half.

Coconut Italian Soda

In a 16 oz. glass (cold cup) add:

2 1/2 oz.	Coconut Italian style syrup
Ice	To fill glass 3/4 full

Fill remainder of glass with club soda. Blend. Top with whipped cream.

Amalfis: Add 1 oz. of Half and Half. (float on top)
Cremosa: Blend in 1 oz. of Half and Half.

Coffee Italian Soda

In a 16 oz. glass (cold cup) add:

  2 1/2 oz. Coffee Italian style syrup
  Ice   To fill glass 3/4 full

Fill remainder of glass with club soda. Blend. Top with whipped cream.

  Amalfis: Add 1 oz. of Half and Half. *(float on top)*
  Cremosa: Blend in 1 oz. of Half and Half.

Coffee 'n' Orange Italian Soda

In a 16 oz. glass (cold cup) add:

  2 oz.   Coffee Italian style syrup
  1/2 oz. Orange Italian style syrup
  Ice   To fill glass 3/4 full

Fill remainder of glass with club soda. Blend. Top with whipped cream.

  Amalfis: Add 1 oz. of Half and Half. *(float on top)*
  Cremosa: Blend in 1 oz. of Half and Half.

Coffee Rumba Italian Soda

In a 16 oz. glass (cold cup) add:

  2 oz.   Coffee Italian style syrup
  1/2 oz. Rum Italian style syrup
  Ice   To fill glass 3/4 full

Fill remainder of glass with club soda. Blend. Top with whipped cream.

  Amalfis: Add 1 oz. of Half and Half. *(float on top)*
  Cremosa: Blend in 1 oz. of Half and Half.

Chocolate Mint Italian Soda

In a 16 oz. glass (cold cup) add:

  2 oz.   Chocolate mint Italian style syrup
  Ice   To fill glass 3/4 full

Fill remainder of glass with club soda. Blend. Top with whipped cream.

  Amalfis: Add 1 oz. of Half and Half. *(float on top)*
  Cremosa: Blend in 1 oz. of Half and Half.

Crab Apple Surprise Italian Soda

In a 16 oz. glass (cold cup) add:

1 1/2 oz.	Apple Italian style syrup
1 oz.	Lemon Italian style syrup
Ice	To fill glass 3/4 full

Fill remainder of glass with club soda. Blend. Top with whipped cream.

Amalfis: Add 1 oz. of Half and Half. (float on top)
Cremosa: Blend in 1 oz. of Half and Half.

Creme de Cacao 'n' Coconut Italian Soda

In a 16 oz. glass (cold cup) add:

2 oz.	Creme de cacao Italian style syrup
1/2 oz.	Coconut Italian style syrup
Ice	To fill glass 3/4 full

Fill remainder of glass with club soda. Blend. Top with whipped cream.

Amalfis: Add 1 oz. of Half and Half. (float on top)
Cremosa: Blend in 1 oz. of Half and Half.

Creme de Cacao 'n' Coffee Italian Soda

In a 16 oz. glass (cold cup) add:

2 oz.	Creme de cacao Italian style syrup
1/2 oz.	Coffee Italian style syrup
Ice	To fill glass 3/4 full

Fill remainder of glass with club soda. Blend. Top with whipped cream.

Amalfis: Add 1 oz. of Half and Half. (float on top)
Cremosa: Blend in 1 oz. of Half and Half.

Creme de Cacao 'n' Irish Cream Italian Soda

In a 16 oz. glass (cold cup) add:

2 oz.	Creme de cacao Italian style syrup
1/2 oz.	Irish cream Italian style syrup
Ice	To fill glass 3/4 full

Fill remainder of glass with club soda. Blend. Top with whipped cream.

Amalfis: Add 1 oz. of Half and Half. (float on top)
Cremosa: Blend in 1 oz. of Half and Half.

Egg Nog Italian Soda

In a 16 oz. glass (cold cup) add:

2 oz.	Egg Nog Italian style syrup
1/2 oz.	Cinnamon Italian style syrup
Ice	To fill glass 3/4 full

Fill remainder of glass with club soda. Blend. Top with whipped cream.

Amalfis: Add 1 oz. of Half and Half. (float on top)
Cremosa: Blend in 1 oz. of Half and Half.

Ginger Italian Soda

In a 16 oz. glass (cold cup) add:

2 oz.	Ginger Italian style syrup
Ice	To fill glass 3/4 full

Fill remainder of glass with club soda. Blend. Top with whipped cream.

Amalfis: Add 1 oz. of Half and Half. (float on top)
Cremosa: Blend in 1 oz. of Half and Half.

Grape Italian Soda

In a 16 oz. glass (cold cup) add:

2 oz.	Grape Italian style syrup
Ice	To fill glass 3/4 full

Fill remainder of glass with club soda. Blend. Top with whipped cream.

Amalfis: Add 1 oz. of Half and Half. (float on top)
Cremosa: Blend in 1 oz. of Half and Half.

Grape Fruit Italian Soda

In a 16 oz. glass (cold cup) add:

2 oz.	Grape fruit Italian style syrup
Ice	To fill glass 3/4 full

Fill remainder of glass with club soda. Blend. Top with whipped cream.

Amalfis: Add 1 oz. of Half and Half. (float on top)
Cremosa: Blend in 1 oz. of Half and Half.

Grenadine Italian Soda

In a 16 oz. glass (cold cup) add:

2 oz.	Grenadine Italian style syrup
Ice	To fill glass 3/4 full

Fill remainder of glass with club soda. Blend. Top with whipped cream.

Amalfis: Add 1 oz. of Half and Half. (float on top)
Cremosa: Blend in 1 oz. of Half and Half.

Irish Cream Italian Soda

In a 16 oz. glass (cold cup) add:

2 oz.	Irish cream Italian style syrup
Ice	To fill glass 3/4 full

Fill remainder of glass with club soda. Blend. Top with whipped cream.

Amalfis: Add 1 oz. of Half and Half. (float on top)
Cremosa: Blend in 1 oz. of Half and Half.

Irish Cream Rumba Italian Soda

In a 16 oz. glass (cold cup) add:

1 1/2 oz.	Irish cream Italian style syrup
1/2 oz.	Rum Italian style syrup
Ice	To fill glass 3/4 full

Fill remainder of glass with club soda. Blend. Top with whipped cream.

Amalfis: Add 1 oz. of Half and Half. (float on top)
Cremosa: Blend in 1 oz. of Half and Half.

Key Lime Pie Italian Soda

In a 16 oz. glass (cold cup) add:

1 1/2 oz.	Lime Italian style syrup
1 oz.	Vanilla Italian style syrup
Ice	To fill glass 3/4 full

Fill remainder of glass with club soda. Blend. Top with whipped cream.

Amalfis: Add 1 oz. of Half and Half. (float on top)
Cremosa: Blend in 1 oz. of Half and Half.

Kiwi Italian Soda

In a 16 oz. glass (cold cup) add:

    2 oz.   Kiwi Italian style syrup
    Ice   To fill glass 3/4 full

Fill remainder of glass with club soda. Blend. Top with whipped cream.

    Amalfis: Add 1 oz. of Half and Half. (float on top)
    Cremosa: Blend in 1 oz. of Half and Half.

Lemon Lime Italian Soda

In a 16 oz. glass (cold cup) add:

    1 1/4 oz.   Lemon Italian style syrup
    1 1/4 oz.   Lime Italian style syrup
    Ice   To fill glass 3/4 full

Fill remainder of glass with club soda. Blend. Top with whipped cream.

    Amalfis: Add 1 oz. of Half and Half. (float on top)
    Cremosa: Blend in 1 oz. of Half and Half.

Lemon Chiffon Cream Pie Italian Soda

In a 16 oz. glass (cold cup) add:

    1 1/2 oz.   Lemon Italian style syrup
    1 oz.   Vanilla Italian style syrup
    Ice   To fill glass 3/4 full

Fill remainder of glass with club soda. Blend. Top with whipped cream.

    Amalfis: Add 1 oz. of Half and Half. (float on top)
    Cremosa: Blend in 1 oz. of Half and Half.

Mango Italian Soda

In a 16 oz. glass (cold cup) add:

    2 oz.   Mango Italian style syrup
    Ice   To fill glass 3/4 full

Fill remainder of glass with club soda. Blend. Top with whipped cream.

    Amalfis: Add 1 oz. of Half and Half. (float on top)
    Cremosa: Blend in 1 oz. of Half and Half.

Mango Kiwi Kiss Italian Soda

In a 16 oz. glass (cold cup) add:

1/2 oz.	Mango Italian style syrup
1/2 oz.	Kiwi Italian style syrup
Ice	To fill glass 3/4 full

Fill remainder of glass with club soda. Blend. Top with whipped cream.

Amalfis: Add 1 oz. of Half and Half. (float on top)
Cremosa: Blend in 1 oz. of Half and Half.

Melon Italian Soda

In a 16 oz. glass (cold cup) add:

2 1/2 oz.	Melon Italian style syrup
Ice	To fill glass 3/4 full

Fill remainder of glass with club soda. Blend. Top with whipped cream.

Amalfis: Add 1 oz. of Half and Half. (float on top)
Cremosa: Blend in 1 oz. of Half and Half.

Orange Vanilla Italian Soda

In a 16 oz. glass (cold cup) add:

2 oz.	Orange Italian style syrup
1/2 oz.	Vanilla Italian style syrup
Ice	To fill glass 3/4 full

Fill remainder of glass with club soda. Blend. Top with whipped cream.

Amalfis: Add 1 oz. of Half and Half. (float on top)
Cremosa: Blend in 1 oz. of Half and Half.

Passion Fruit Italian Soda

In a 16 oz. glass (cold cup) add:

2 1/2 oz.	Passion fruit Italian style syrup
Ice	To fill glass 3/4 full

Fill remainder of glass with club soda. Blend. Top with whipped cream.

Amalfis: Add 1 oz. of Half and Half. (float on top)
Cremosa: Blend in 1 oz. of Half and Half.

Peach Nut Italian Soda

In a 16 oz. glass (cold cup) add:

1 1/2 oz.	Peach Italian style syrup
1/2 oz.	Almond Italian style syrup
Ice	To fill glass 3/4 full

Fill remainder of glass with club soda. Blend. Top with whipped cream.

Amalfis: Add 1 oz. of Half and Half. (float on top)
Cremosa: Blend in 1 oz. of Half and Half.

Pina Colada Italian Soda

In a 16 oz. glass (cold cup) add:

1 oz.	Coconut Italian style syrup*
1/2 oz.	Pineapple Italian style syrup*
1/2 oz.	Rum Italian style syrup
Ice	To fill glass 3/4 full

*Or use 1 oz. Pina Colada Italian style syrup as a substitute for both of these

Fill remainder of glass with club soda. Blend. Top with whipped cream.

Amalfis: Add 1 oz. of Half and Half. (float on top)
Cremosa: Blend in 1 oz. of Half and Half.

Popcorn Italian Soda

In a 16 oz. glass (cold cup) add:

1 3/4 oz.	Peach Italian style syrup
1/2 oz.	Hazelnut Italian style syrup
Ice	To fill glass 3/4 full

Fill remainder of glass with club soda. Blend. Top with whipped cream.

Amalfis: Add 1 oz. of Half and Half. (float on top)
Cremosa: Blend in 1 oz. of Half and Half.

Raspberry Italian Soda

In a 16 oz. glass (cold cup) add:

2 oz.	Raspberry Italian style syrup
Ice	To fill glass 3/4 full

Fill remainder of glass with club soda. Blend. Top with whipped cream.

Amalfis: Add 1 oz. of Half and Half. (float on top)
Cremosa: Blend in 1 oz. of Half and Half.

Raspberry Sour Cream Pie Italian Soda

In a 16 oz. glass (cold cup) add:

1 1/2 oz.	Raspberry Italian style syrup
1 oz.	Lemon Italian style syrup
Ice	To fill glass 3/4 full

Fill remainder of glass with club soda. Blend. Top with whipped cream.

Amalfis: Add 1 oz. of Half and Half. (float on top)
Cremosa: Blend in 1 oz. of Half and Half.

Root Beer Italian Soda

In a 16 oz. glass (cold cup) add:

2 oz.	Root beer Italian style syrup
Ice	To fill glass 3/4 full

Fill remainder of glass with club soda. Blend. Top with whipped cream.

Amalfis: Add 1 oz. of Half and Half. (float on top)
Cremosa: Blend in 1 oz. of Half and Half.

Strawberry Italian Soda

In a 16 oz. glass (cold cup) add:

2 oz.	Strawberry Italian style syrup
Ice	To fill glass 3/4 full

Fill remainder of glass with club soda. Blend. Top with whipped cream.

Amalfis: Add 1 oz. of Half and Half. (float on top)
Cremosa: Blend in 1 oz. of Half and Half.

Strawberry Watermelon Italian Soda

In a 16 oz. glass (cold cup) add:

1 oz.	Strawberry Italian style syrup
1 oz.	Watermelon Italian style syrup
Ice	To fill glass 3/4 full

Fill remainder of glass with club soda. Blend. Top with whipped cream.

Amalfis: Add 1 oz. of Half and Half. (float on top)
Cremosa: Blend in 1 oz. of Half and Half.

Strawberry Lime Twist Italian Soda

In a 16 oz. glass (cold cup) add:

1 oz.	Strawberry Italian style syrup
1 oz.	Lime Italian style syrup
1/2 oz.	Amaretto Italian style syrup
Ice	To fill glass 3/4 full

Fill remainder of glass with club soda. Blend. Top with whipped cream.

Amalfis: Add 1 oz. of Half and Half. (float on top)
Cremosa: Blend in 1 oz. of Half and Half.

Watermelon Italian Soda

In a 16 oz. glass (cold cup) add:

2 oz.	Watermelon Italian style syrup
Ice	To fill glass 3/4 full

Fill remainder of glass with club soda. Blend. Top with whipped cream.

Amalfis: Add 1 oz. of Half and Half. (float on top)
Cremosa: Blend in 1 oz. of Half and Half.

Watermelon Kiwi Italian Soda

In a 16 oz. glass (cold cup) add:

1 1/2 oz.	Watermelon Italian style syrup
1/2 oz.	Kiwi Italian style syrup
Ice	To fill glass 3/4 full

Fill remainder of glass with club soda. Blend. Top with whipped cream.

Amalfis: Add 1 oz. of Half and Half. (float on top)
Cremosa: Blend in 1 oz. of Half and Half.

Watermelon Raspberry Italian Soda

In a 16 oz. glass (cold cup) add:

1 1/2 oz.	Watermelon Italian style syrup
1/2 oz.	Raspberry Italian style syrup
Ice	To fill glass 3/4 full

Fill remainder of glass with club soda. Blend. Top with whipped cream.

Amalfis: Add 1 oz. of Half and Half. (float on top)
Cremosa: Blend in 1 oz. of Half and Half.

Vanilla Italian Soda

In a 16 oz. glass (cold cup) add:

2 oz.	Vanilla Italian style syrup
Ice	To fill glass 3/4 full

Fill remainder of glass with club soda. Blend. Top with whipped cream.

Amalfis: Add 1 oz. of Half and Half. (float on top)
Cremosa: Blend in 1 oz. of Half and Half.

ITALIAN SMOOTHIES

BASIC ITALIAN SMOOTHIE RECIPE

2 oz.	Syrup flavor of choice
2 oz.	Half and Half
2 oz.	Club soda
8	1 oz. ice cubes

In a blender, combine the above ingredients. Crush until smooth. Pour into serving glass. Top with whipped cream, and garnish. Makes 16 oz.

Italian
Style
Syrup

Ice Cube Tray

Blender

Cherry Vanilla Italian Smoothie

1 oz.	Cherry Italian style syrup
1 oz.	Vanilla Italian style syrup
2 oz.	Half and Half
2 oz.	Club soda
8	1 oz. ice cubes

In a blender, combine the above ingredients. Crush until smooth. Pour into serving glass. Top with whipped cream, and garnish with colorful sprinkles.

Coffee Italian Smoothie

2 oz.	Coffee Italian style syrup
2 oz.	Half and Half
2 oz.	Club soda
8	1 oz. ice cubes

In a blender, combine the above ingredients. Crush until smooth. Pour into serving glass. Top with whipped cream, and dust with cinnamon.

Cranberry Cinnamon Italian Smoothie

1 oz.	Cranberry Italian style syrup
1 oz.	Cinnamon Italian style syrup
2 oz.	Half and Half
2 oz.	Club soda
8	1 oz. ice cubes

In a blender, combine the above ingredients. Crush until smooth. Pour into serving glass. Top with whipped cream, and dust with cinnamon.

Cranberry Raspberry Italian Smoothie

1 oz.	Cranberry Italian style syrup
1 oz.	Raspberry Italian style syrup
2 oz.	Half and Half
2 oz.	Club soda
8	1 oz. ice cubes

In a blender, combine the above ingredients. Crush until smooth. Pour into serving glass. Top with whipped cream, and garnish with raspberry-sugar granules.

Creme de Cacao & Irish Cream Italian Smoothie

1 oz.	Creme de cacao Italian style syrup
1 oz.	Irish cream Italian style syrup
2 oz.	Half and Half
2 oz.	Club soda
8	1 oz. ice cubes

In a blender, combine the above ingredients. Crush until smooth. Pour into serving glass. Top with whipped cream, and garnish with chocolate sprinkles.

Irish Cream Italian Smoothie

1 oz.	Irish cream Italian style syrup
2 oz.	Half and Half
2 oz.	Club soda
8	1 oz. ice cubes

In a blender, combine the above ingredients. Crush until smooth. Pour into serving glass. Top with whipped cream.

Lemon Lime Italian Smoothie

1 oz.	Lemon Italian style syrup
1 oz.	Lime Italian style syrup
2 oz.	Half and Half
2 oz.	Club soda
8	1 oz. ice cubes

In a blender, combine the above ingredients. Crush until smooth. Pour into serving glass. Top with whipped cream, and garnish with lemon or lime slices.

Orange & Vanilla Italian Smoothie

1 oz.	Orange Italian style syrup
1 oz.	Vanilla Italian style syrup
2 oz.	Half and Half
2 oz.	Club soda
8	1 oz. ice cubes

In a blender, combine the above ingredients. Crush until smooth. Pour into serving glass. Top with whipped cream, and garnish with a slice of orange.

Raspberry Vanilla Italian Smoothie

1 oz.	Raspberry Italian style syrup
1 oz.	Vanilla Italian style syrup
2 oz.	Half and Half
2 oz.	Club soda
8	1oz. ice cubes

In a blender, combine the above ingredients. Crush until smooth. Pour into serving glass. Top with whipped cream, and garnish with raspberry-sugar granules.

Strawberry Watermelon Italian Smoothie

1 oz.	Strawberry Italian style syrup
1 oz.	Watermelon Italian style syrup
2 oz.	Half and Half
2 oz.	Club soda
8	1 oz. ice cubes

In a blender, combine the above ingredients. Crush until smooth. Pour into serving glass. Top with whipped cream, and garnish with a strawberry slice.

Pina Colada Italian Smoothie

1/2 oz.	Rum Italian style syrup
1/2 oz.	Pineapple Italian style syrup*
1 oz.	Coconut Italian style syrup*
2 oz.	Half and Half
2 oz.	Club soda
8	1 oz. ice cubes

*Or use 1 1/2 oz. Pina Colada Italian style syrup as a substitute for both of these.

In a blender, combine the above ingredients. Crush until smooth. Pour into serving glass. Top with whipped cream, and garnish with a pineapple slice.

MISCELLANEOUS DRINKS

Creamcicle

In a 16 oz. glass (cold cup) combine:

    1 oz.   Vanilla Italian style syrup
    10 oz.   Orange juice
    1 oz.   Half and Half

Blend. Fill remainder of glass with ice. Top with whipped cream, garnish with an orange slice.

Tropicolada

In a 16 oz. glass (cold cup) combine:

    1/2 oz.   Vanilla Italian style syrup
    1/2 oz.   Coconut Italian style syrup
    1/4 oz.   Rum Italian style syrup
    10 oz.   Orange juice
    1 oz.   Half and Half

Blend. Fill remainder of glass with ice. Top with whipped cream, garnish with a fresh fruit kabob.

Island Cooler

In a 16 oz. glass (cold cup) combine:

    3/4 oz.   Vanilla Italian style syrup
    1/4 oz.   Rum Italian style syrup
    10 oz.   Orange/Pineapple juice
    1 oz.   Half and Half

Blend. Fill remainder of glass with ice. Top with whipped cream, garnish with a fresh fruit kabob.

GRANITAS

· ·

What makes this drink so special is the concentrated taste that one experiences from its cool sweet crystals. I like to call this unique semi-frozen drink, an adult form of a slushy.

The granita drink is dispensed from the granitore machine. This special machine, developed for this type of product, maintains the liquid base at freezing temperatures. Here's where the magic happens, as the drink mix begins to freeze there are blades that rotate, scraping it from the sides of the barrel. With the right concentration of sugar (sugar acts as an anti-freeze) the product is maintained at a texture that is smooth and grainy with crystal like beads.

The granita, when made correctly is a slushy type drink with a crystal, grainy texture that is full of sweetness and taste.

There are now many new products on the market for making granitas. These base mixes are balanced with the right amount of sugar and usually come in a concentrated form, that is then combined with a liquid, according to the manufacturers instructions.

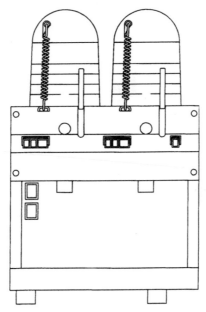

Granita Machine (Granitore)

Granita

Garnish —

Whipped Topping

Flavored Syrup

Latté Granita

16 oz. glass (cold cup)

For making the latté granitas, you can use a prepared concentrate and mix according to the manufactures instructions. Or you can make your own latte base by using fresh espresso that you've brewed.

LATTÉ GRANITA BASE RECIPE

1 1/4	Cups sugar
24 oz.	Espresso
1 gal.	Milk (your choice of milk)

In a two gallon container, dissolve the sugar with the warm espresso. Add the milk and stir. Pour about 1/2 of the mix into your granita machine. As the mix begins to freeze add small amounts of the latte mix, until you have what is needed in the barrel. Refrigerate any unused portion of the mix. **(For larger quanities, this recipe can be doubled)**

Amaretto Latté Granita

In a 16 oz. glass combine:

15 1/2 oz.   Latté granita
1/2 oz.   Amaretto Italian style syrup

Stir until blended. Top with whipped cream.

Cinnamon Latté Granita

In a 16 oz. glass combine:

15 1/2 oz.   Latté Granita
1/2 oz.   Cinnamon Italian style syrup

Stir until blended. Top with whipped cream, dust with a dash of cinnamon and garnish with a cinnamon stick.

Coffee 'n' Cream Latté Granita

In a 16 oz. glass combine:

14 oz.   Latté Granita
1/2 oz.   Coffee Italian style syrup
1 1/2 oz.   Half and Half

Stir until blended. Top with whipped cream.

Ginger Cream Latté Granita

In a 16 oz. glass combine:

15 1/2 oz.   Latté granita
1/2 oz.   Ginger Italian style syrup

Stir until blended. Top with whipped cream and garnish with a ginger snap cookie.

Hazelnut Latté Granita

In a 16 oz. glass combine:

15 1/2 oz.   Latté granita
1/2 oz.   Hazelnut Italian style syrup

Stir until blended. Top with whipped cream.

Mint Julep Latté Granita

In a 16 oz. glass combine:

15 1/2 oz.   Latté granita
1/2 oz.   Mint Italian style syrup

Stir until blended. Top with whipped cream and garnish with a sprig of mint.

Ozark Black Walnut Pie Latté Granita

In a 16 oz. glass combine:

14 oz.	Latté granita
1/2 oz.	Toasted Walnut Italian style syrup
1 1/2 oz.	Half and Half

Stir until blended. Top with whipped cream and garnish with a walnut half.

Praline Latté Granita

In a 16 oz. glass combine:

15 1/2 oz.	Latté granita
1/2 oz.	Praline Italian style syrup

Stir until blended. Top with whipped cream.

Raspberry 'n' Cream Latté Granita

In a 16 oz. glass combine:

15 1/2 oz.	Latté granita
1/2 oz.	Raspberry Italian style syrup

Stir until blended. Top with whipped cream.

Rum Latté Granita

In a 16 oz. glass combine:

15 1/2 oz.	Latté granita
1/2 oz.	Amaretto Italian style syrup

Stir until blended. Top with whipped cream.

For my fruit granitas I used a lemonade (lemon ice) granita base. Mixed it according to the manufacturers instructions, and poured the amount needed into my machine. Use this prepared mix as a base to create the recipes in this section.

By combining the various fruit flavored Italian style syrups with the prepared lemonade mix, freshly dispensed from the granita machine. I used this base recipe as a guideline.

LEMONADE GRANITA BASE RECIPE

In a 16 oz. glass combine;

13 oz.	lemonade granita mix
1 oz.	fruit flavored Italian style syrup
1 oz.	half and half (optional)

Stir and blend ingredients Top with whipped cream and garnish with fruit slices.

Apple Sour Cream Pie Granita

In a 16 oz. glass combine:

13 oz.	Lemonade granita
1 oz.	Apple Italian style syrup
1 oz.	Half and Half

Stir until blended. Top with whipped cream and sprinkle with a dash of nutmeg.

Blackberry Sour Cream Pie Granita

In a 16 oz. glass combine:

13 oz.	Lemonade granita
1 oz.	Blackberry Italian style syrup
1 oz.	Half and Half

Stir until blended. Top with whipped cream and drizzle with a small amount of the blackberry syrup.

Blueberries 'n' Cream Granita

In a 16 oz. glass combine:

13 oz.	Lemonade granita
1 oz.	Blueberry Italian style syrup
1 oz.	Half and Half

Stir until blended. Top with whipped cream and garnish with several blueberries.

Boysenberries 'n' Cream Granita

In a 16 oz. glass combine:

    13 oz.   Lemonade granita
    1 oz.   Boysenberry Italian style syrup
    1 oz.   Half and Half

Stir until blended. Top with whipped cream and drizzle with a small amount of the boysenberry syrup.

Bing Cherry Jubilee Granita

In a 16 oz. glass combine:

    13 oz.   Lemonade granita
    1 oz.   New England black cherry Italian style syrup
    1 oz.   Half and Half

Stir until blended. Top with whipped cream, drizzle with small amount of the black cherry syrup and garnish with a bing cherry.

Cherry Pie Granita

In a 16 oz. glass combine:

    13 oz.   Lemonade granita
    1 oz.   Cherry Italian style syrup
    1 oz.   Half and Half

Stir until blended. Top with whipped cream and garnish with a maraschino cherry.

Cranberry Tart Granita

In a 16 oz. glass combine:

    13 oz.   Lemonade granita
    1 oz.   Cranberry Italian style syrup
    1 oz.   Half and Half

Stir until blended. Top with whipped cream and dust with a small amount of cinnamon.

Grape Punch Granita

In a 16 oz. glass combine:

    13 oz.   Lemonade granita
    1 oz.   Grape Italian style syrup
    1 oz.   Half and Half

Stir until blended. Top with whipped cream and garnish with multi-colored sprinkles.

Hawaiian Punch Granita

In a 16 oz. glass combine:

      13 oz.   Lemonade granita
      1/2 oz.   Pineapple Italian style syrup
      1/2 oz.   Passion fruit Italian style syrup
      1 oz.   Half and Half

Stir until blended. Top with whipped cream and garnish with pineapple slices.

Kiwi Kiss Granita

In a 16 oz. glass combine:

      13 oz.   Lemonade granita
      1 oz.   Kiwi Italian style syrup
      1 oz.   Half and Half

Stir until blended. Top with whipped cream and garnish with kiwi slices.

Key Lime Pie Granita

In a 16 oz. glass combine:

      13 oz.   Lemonade granita
      1 oz.   Lime Italian style syrup
      1 oz.   Half and Half

Stir until blended. Top with whipped cream and garnish with a slice of lime.

Lemon Chiffon Granita

In a 16 oz. glass combine:

      13 oz.   Lemonade granita
      1 oz.   Lemon Italian style syrup
      1 oz.   Half and Half

Stir until blended. Top with whipped cream and garnish with a lemon slice.

Mango Chiffon Granita

In a 16 oz. glass combine:

      13 oz.   Lemonade granita
      1 oz.   Mango Italian style syrup
      1 oz.   Half and Half

Stir until blended. Top with whipped cream and drizzle with a small amount of the mango syrup.

Orange Chiffon Granita

In a 16 oz. glass combine:

      13 oz.   Lemonade granita
      1 oz.   Orange Italian style syrup
      1 oz.   Half and Half

Stir until blended. Top with whipped cream and garnish with an orange slice.

Passion Fruit Granita

In a 16 oz. glass combine:

      13 oz.   Lemonade granita
      1 oz.   Passion fruit Italian style syrup
      1 oz.   Half and Half

Stir until blended. Top with whipped cream and garnish with a maraschino cherry.

Peach Parfait Granita

In a 16 oz. glass combine:

      13 oz.   Lemonade granita
      1 oz.   Peach Italian style syrup
      1 oz.   Half and Half

Stir until blended. Top with whipped cream and dust lightly with cinnamon.

Raspberry Sour Cream Pie Granita

In a 16 oz. glass combine:

      13 oz.   Lemonade granita
      1 oz.   Raspberry Italian style syrup
      1 oz.   Half and Half

Stir until blended. Top with whipped cream and garnish with a few raspberries.

Strawberry Daiquiri Granita

In a 16 oz. glass combine:

      13 oz.   Lemonade granita
      1 oz.   Strawberry Italian style syrup
      1 oz.   Half and Half

Stir until blended. Top with whipped cream and garnish with a strawberry slice.

Watermelon Medley Granita

In a 16 oz. glass combine:

13 oz.	Lemonade granita
1 oz.	Watermelon Italian style syrup
1 oz.	Half and Half

Stir until blended. Top with whipped cream and drizzle with a small amount of the Watermelon syrup.

HOMESTYLE GRANITAS

Commercial granitas require high quanities of sugar in order for the granita mixture to properly crystallize without freezing solid.

The great advantage to making homestyle granitas is that you can control the amount of sugar or sweetener used, and with the milk of your choice.

When I first started playing around with making granitas at home, I had no idea how successful these drinks would be. The quality of the taste and texture is very similar to that of a commercial granita, but here again without all the sugar.

Blender

Ice Cube Tray

IN MAKING OUR HOMESTYLE GRANITAS WE USED:

Shots that equaled 1 3/4 oz. of espresso.

2% milk.

1oz. ice cubes. (*our ice cube tray made 14, one ounce ice cubes*)

Seven 1oz. espresso ice cubes combined with 2/3 cup cold milk, crushed and blended makes enough product to fill one, 16oz. glass or two 8oz. glasses.

Homestyle Espresso Granita
. . . .

Mix 8 oz. of espresso with 6 oz. cold water, (sweeten to taste, if desired). Freeze into ice cubes.

In blender crush 7 of these espresso cubes with 2/3 cup cold water. Blend until smooth, pour into serving glass(s).

OPTION: *Top with whipped cream or drizzle with half and half.*

Homestyle Espresso and Cream Granita
. . . .

Mix 8 oz. espresso with 6 oz. cold water, (sweeten to taste, if desired). Freeze into ice cubes.

In blender crush 7 of these espresso cubes with 2/3 cup cold half and half*. Blend until smooth, pour into serving glass(s).

*For a flavored variety substitute one of the flavored non-dairy coffee creamers. (Irish cream, Amaretto, French Vanilla Etc.) These creamers may be diluted with equal parts of milk.

Homestyle Almond Latté Granita

2 oz.	Almond Italian style syrup
2 shots	Espresso
8 1/2 oz.	Cold milk

Combine ingredients then freeze into ice cubes. In a blender crush 7 of these Latté cubes with 2/3 cup cold milk. Blend until smooth. Pour into serving glass(s). Top with whipped cream and powdered almond.

Homestyle Amaretto Latté Granita

2 oz.	Amaretto Italian style syrup
2 shots	Espresso
8 1/2 oz.	Cold milk

Combine Ingredients then freeze into ice cubes. In a blender crush 7 of these Latté cubes with 2/3 cup cold milk. Blend until smooth. Pour into serving glass(s). Top with amaretto flavored whipped cream.

Homestyle Banana Coconut Latté Granita

1 oz.	Banana Italian style syrup
1 oz.	Coconut Italian style syrup
2 shots	Espresso
8 1/2 oz.	Cold milk

Combine ingredients then freeze into ice cubes. In a blender crush 7 of these Latté cubes with 2/3 cup cold milk. Blend until smooth. Pour into serving glass(s). Top with whipped cream and garnish with toasted coconut.

Homestyle Banana Mocha Granita

1 1/2 oz.	Chocolate syrup
1/2 oz.	Banana Italian style syrup
2 shots	Espresso
8 1/2 oz.	Cold milk

Combine ingredients then freeze into ice cubes. In a blender crush 7 of these mocha cubes with 2/3 cup cold milk. Blend until smooth. Pour into serving glass(s).

Homestyle Black Walnut Latté Granita

2 oz.	Walnut Italian style syrup
2 shots	Espresso
8 1/2 oz.	Cold milk

Combine ingredients then freeze into ice cubes. In a blender crush 7 of these Latté cubes with 2/3 cup cold milk. Blend until smooth. Pour into serving glass(s). Top with whipped cream and garnish with a teaspoon of crushed walnuts.

Homestyle Cherry Mocha Granita

1 1/2 oz.	Chocolate syrup
1/2 oz.	Cherry Italian style syrup
2 shots	Espresso
8 1/2 oz.	Cold milk

Combine ingredients then freeze into ice cubes. In a blender crush 7 of these mocha cubes with 2/3 cup cold milk. Blend until smooth. Pour into serving glass(s). Top with whipped cream, drizzle with the chocolate syrup and garnish with a maraschino cherry.

Homestyle Cinnamon Latté Granita

2 oz.	Cinnamon Italian style syrup
2 shots	Espresso
8 1/2 oz.	Cold milk

Combine ingredients then freeze into ice cubes. In a blender crush 7 of these Latté ice cubes with 2/3 cup cold milk. Blend until smooth. Pour into serving glass(s). Top with whipped cream and garnish with a cinnamon stick.

Homestyle Coffee Latté Granita

2 oz.	Coffee Italian style syrup
2 shots	Espresso
8 1/2 oz.	Cold milk

Combine ingredients then freeze into ice cubes. In a blender crush 7 of these Latté ice cubes with 2/3 cup cold milk. Blend until smooth. Pour into serving glass(s). Top with whipped cream.

Homestyle Creme de Cacao Latté Granita

2 oz.	Creme de cacao Italian style syrup
2 shots	Espresso
8 1/2 oz.	Cold milk

Combine ingredients then freeze into ice cubes. In a blender crush 7 of these Latté cubes with 2/3 cup cold milk. Blend until smooth. Pour into serving glass(s). Top with whipped cream and dust with cocoa powder.

GRANITA TRIVIA

Try some of the non-fat sugar free Italian style syrups. Create your own combination.

Homestyle Irish Cream Latté Granita

2 oz.	Irish cream Italian style syrup
2 shots	Espresso
8 1/2 oz.	Cold milk

Combine ingredients then freeze into ice cubes. In a blender crush 7 of these Latté cubes with 2/3 cup cold milk. Blend until smooth. Pour into serving glass(s). Top with whipped cream.

Homestyle Irish Cream Mocha Granita

1 oz.	Irish cream Italian style syrup
1 oz.	Chocolate syrup
2 shots	Espresso
8 1/2 oz.	Cold milk

Combine ingredients then freeze into ice cubes. In a blender Crush 7 of these mocha cubes with 2/3 cup cold milk. Blend until smooth. Pour into serving glass(s). Top with whipped cream.

Homestyle Ginger Cream Latté Granita

2 oz.	Ginger Italian style syrup
2 shots	Espresso
8 1/2 oz.	Cold milk

Combine ingredients then freeze into ice cubes. In a blender crush 7 of these Latté cubes with 2/3 cup cold milk. Blend until smooth. Pour into serving glass(s). Top with whipped cream, dust with cinnamon and garnish with a gingersnap cookie.

Homestyle Macadamia Nut Latté Granita

2 oz.	Macadamia nut Italian style syrup
2 shots	Espresso
8 1/2 oz.	Cold milk

Combine ingredients then freeze into ice cubes. In a blender crush 7 of these Latté cubes with 2/3 cup cold milk. Blend until smooth. Pour into serving glass(s). Top with whipped cream and garnish with a macadamia nut.

Homestyle Macadamia Nut Mocha Granita

1 1/2 oz.	Chocolate syrup
1/2 oz.	Macadamia nut Italian style syrup
2 shots	Espresso
8 1/2 oz.	Cold milk

Combine ingredients then freeze into ice cubes. In a blender crush 7 of these mocha cubes with 2/3 cup cold milk. Blend until smooth. Pour into serving glass(s). Top with whipped cream and garnish with a chocolate covered macadamia nut.

Homestyle Mocha Granita

2 oz.	Chocolate syrup
2 shots	Espresso
8 1/2 oz.	Cold milk

Combine ingredients then freeze into ice cubes. In a blender crush 7 of these mocha cubes with 2/3 cup cold milk. Blend until smooth. Pour into serving glass(s). Top with whipped cream and garnish with a chocolate covered espresso bean.

Homestyle Orange Mocha Granita

1 1/2 oz.	Chocolate syrup
1/2 oz.	Orange Italian style syrup
2 shots	Espresso
8 1/2 oz.	Cold milk

Combine ingredients then freeze into ice cubes. In a blender crush 7 of these mocha cubes with 2/3 cup cold milk. Blend until smooth. Pour into serving glass(s). Top with whipped cream and garnish with chocolate sprinkles.

Homestyle Raspberry Latté Granita

2 oz.	Raspberry Italian style syrup
2 shots	Espresso
8 1/2 oz.	Cold milk

Combine ingredients then freeze into ice cubes. In a blender crush 7 of these Latté cubes with 2/3 cup cold milk. Blend until smooth. Pour into serving glass(s). Top with whipped cream and drizzle with the raspberry syrup.

Homestyle Raspberry Walnut Torte Granita

1 oz.	Chocolate syrup
1/2 oz.	Raspberry Italian style syrup
1/2 oz.	Walnut Italian style syrup
2 shots	Espresso
8 1/2 oz.	Cold milk

Combine ingredients then freeze into ice cubes. In a blender crush 7 of these mocha cubes with 2/3 cup cold milk. Blend until smooth. Pour into serving glass(s). Top with whipped cream and garnish with crushed walnuts.

Homestyle Strawberries 'n' Cream Latté Granita

2 oz.	Strawberry Italian style syrup
2 shots	Espresso
8 1/2 oz.	Cold milk

Combine ingredients then freeze into ice cubes. In a blender crush 7 of these Latté cubes with 2/3 cup cold milk. Blend until smooth. Pour into serving glass(s). Top with whipped cream and garnish with chocolate sprinkles.

Homestyle Vanilla Latté Granita

2 oz.	Vanilla Italian style syrup
2 shots	Espresso
8 1/2 oz.	Cold Milk

Combine ingredients then freeze into ice cubes. In a blender crush 7 of these Latté cubes with 2/3 cup cold milk. Blend until smooth. Pour into serving glass(s). Top with whipped cream and dust lightly with cinnamon.

Homestyle Vanilla Nut Latté Granita

1 1/2 oz.	Vanilla Italian style syrup
1/2 oz.	Hazelnut Italian style syrup*
2 shots	Espresso
8 1/2 oz.	Cold milk

*Can substitute with walnut or macadamia nut Italian style syrups

Combine ingredients then freeze into ice cubes. In a blender crush 7 of these Latté cubes with 2/3 cup cold milk. Blend until smooth. Pour into serving glass(s). Top with whipped cream and garnish with crushed hazelnuts.

HOMESTYLE PINK RUBY MIST TEA GRANITA

• •

BASE RECIPE

In a sauce pan, bring one quart of fresh cold tap water to a full rolling boil. Remove from heat, add 8 bags of ruby mist herb tea and let steep for five minutes. Remove the tea bags and cool the tea with 2 cups of cold tap water. Refrigerate until completely cooled.

Combine one 12 oz. can of frozen concentrated pink lemonade with 36 oz. of the cold ruby mist tea. Pour mix into ice cube trays and freeze. Will fill about 4 trays.

HOMESTYLE PINK RUBY MIST TEA GRANITA

In a blender crush 7 of these ruby mist tea ice cubes with 1/2 cup cold water or unused tea. Blend until smooth. Pour into glass(s). Makes about 14 oz.

Blender

Ice Cube Tray

HOMESTYLE FRUIT JUICE GRANITAS

. . . .

Using frozen concentrated fruit juice*, you can create fun, easy, and flavorful homestyle granitas, that the whole family can enjoy.

BASE RECIPE

1-12 oz. can	Frozen concentrated fruit juice (*of your choice*)
2 1/2-12 oz. cans	Cold water (*can be substituted with tea*)

Mix juice concentrate with water. Pour into ice cube trays and freeze. Will fill about 3 ice cube trays.

However, if you choose to use a frozen concentrated lemonade, you will need to add 3 cans of water.

HOMESTYLE FRUIT JUICE GRANITA

7	Fruit juice ice cubes
1/2 cup	Cold water (*can be substituted with tea*)

In blender crush 7 of these fruit juice ice cubes with the 1/2 cup cold water. Blend until smooth. Pour into serving glass(s).

HOMESTYLE LEMON TEA GRANITA

BASE RECIPE

1-12 oz. can	Frozen concentrated lemonade
3-12 oz. cans	Cold Tea*

Mix ingredients until the lemonade is dissolved. Pour into ice cube trays and freeze. Will fill about 4 ice cube trays. In a blender crush 7 of these lemon tea ice cubes with 1/2 cup cold water. Blend until smooth. Pour into serving glass(s).

*See section for brewing tea.

With these lemon tea ice cubes combined with an Italian style syrup, you can be creative and develop your own recipe or use one of the following.

Homestyle Bing Cherry Lemon Tea Granita

   1 oz.   Black cherry Italian style syrup
   1/2 cup Cold water or tea
   7   Lemon tea ice cubes

In a blender crush ingredients until smooth. Pour into glass(s). Garnish with a bing cherry.

Homestyle Blackberry Lemon Tea Granita

   1 oz.   Blackberry Italian style syrup
   1/2 cup Cold water or tea
   7   Lemon tea ice cubes

In a blender crush ingredients until smoooth. Pour into glass(s). Garnish with a slice of lemon.

Homestyle Boysenberry Lemon Tea Granita

   1 oz.   Boysenberry Italian style syrup
   1/2 cup Cold water or tea
   7   Lemon tea ice cubes

In a blender crush ingredients until smooth. Pour into glass(s). Garnish with a slice of lemon.

Homestyle Cherry Lemon Tea Granita

   1 oz.   Cherry Italian style syrup
   1/2 cup Cold water or tea
   7   Lemon tea ice cubes

In a blender crush ingredients until smooth. Pour into glass(s). Garnish with a maraschino cherry.

Homestyle Cherry Nut Lemon Tea Granita

   3/4 oz. Cherry Italian style syrup
   1/2 oz. Almond Italian style syrup
   1/2 cup Cold water or Tea
   7   Lemon tea ice cubes

In a blender crush ingredients until smooth. Pour into glass(s). Garnish with a maraschino cherry.

Homestyle Huckleberry Lemon Tea Granita

l oz.	Huckleberry Italian style syrup
1/2 cup	Cold water or tea
7	Lemon tea ice cubes

In a blender crush ingredients until smooth. Pour into glass(s). Garnish with a lemon slice.

Homestyle Huckleberry Almond Lemon Tea Granita

3/4 oz.	Huckleberry Italian style syrup
1/2 oz.	Almond Italian style syrup
1/2 cup	Cold water or tea
7	Lemon tea ice cubes

In a blender crush ingredients until smooth. Pour into glass(s). Garnish with a lemon slice.

Homestyle Kiwi Lemon Tea Granita

l oz.	Kiwi Italian style syrup
1/2 cup	Cold water or tea
7	Lemon tea ice cubes

In a blender crush ingredients until smooth. Pour into glass(s). Garnish with a kiwi slice.

Homestyle Mango Lemon Tea Granita

l oz.	Mango Italian style syrup
1/2 oz.	Cold water or tea
7	Lemon tea ice cubes

In a blender crush ingredients until smooth. Pour into glass(s). Garnsh with a slice of lemon.

To Tea or to La Tea?

TEA

· ·

Green, Oolong and Black tea all come from the tea plant called Camellia sinensis. Like coffee, the taste and quality of the tea will vary depending on the region, elevation, soil, climate and weather conditions in which it has been grown.

Once the tea leaves have been harvested, it is then the method of processing that will determine which of the teas it will become.

Black tea (such as Lipton) is withered and fermented longer than oolong tea, these teas are called fermented teas. Green tea, known as unfermented tea, is the least processed of the three teas.

Blending, processing and grading teas, is an art much like blending and roasting different coffee beans. Teas are often blended with teas from other regions, flavored with extracts, spices and herbs to create new varieties.

THE THREE MUSKATEAS

Green Tea

Black Tea

Oolong Tea

TEA TRIVIA

The tea plant is a bush that if left unpruned can grow over 50 feet tall. But when maintained for harvesting is kept at about 5-6 feet.

The tea garden as it is called, may exceed areas over hundreds of acres.

Know how old your tea is, tea has a longer shelf life than coffee.

Bothered by nausea or an upset stomach? Try a cup of warm tea.

Moist tea leaves can be used to soothe insect bites.

To help maintain good strong bones, you need to eat or drink foods that contain manganese, and tea is a good source.

Tea contains fluoride, green tea has the most.

Drinking tea can help promote healthy arteries.

Recent studies have shown that diets rich in green tea show a reduced arterial blockage.

Green tea, Oolong tea and Black tea all have anticancer effects. Green tea contains the most. The other teas loose some of their effect while being processed.

Green tea contains the most anticancer substances called catechins.

To some, drinking 4 or 5 cups of tea a day may be as beneficial as eating fruits and vegetables.

REMEMBER HEARING ONE OF THESE?

Not for all the tea in China: No matter what the price, it's not for sale.

Teetotal: A teetotaler is a person who is abstaining from drinking alcoholic beverages.

That's another cup of tea: That's a different story

GUIDELINES FOR BREWING A PERFECT POT OF TEA

Start with a clean tea kettle and tea pot. Use fresh cold water. Bring water to a full rolling boil (212° F). Don't boil water too long, it will begin to lose oxygen which may effect the taste of your tea. Pour the boiling water directly onto the tea bag(s). If using a tea pot, warm the pot before steeping the tea. (Know your tea, how many tea bags will you need for your tea pot or cup of tea. One tea bag will not flavor a 16 oz. mug.) Steep the tea for the proper amount of time. Color does not indicate that the tea is ready. Add sweetener or other flavors after the tea has finished brewing.

BREWING THE PERFECT ICE TEA

Stove top method I: In a sauce pan bring 1 quart of fresh cold water to a full rolling boil. Remove from heat, add 8 tea bags and let steep for 4 minutes. Remove the tea bags, add 1 quart fresh cold water to cool the tea. Refrigerate. Makes two quarts.

Stove top method II: In a sauce pan bring 2 quarts of fresh cold water to a full rolling boil. Remove from heat, add 8 tea bags , and let steep for 4 minutes. Remove the tea bags, cover pan and let cool to room temperature then refrigerate.

Instant Iced Tea Method: Combine 3 heaping tablespoons of un-sweetened instant iced tea, with 2 quarts cold water. Or, follow the manufacturers instructions. Refrigerate.

Sun Tea Method: Fill a glass container with 2 quarts fresh cold water, add 8-10 tea bags. Place in the sun and let brew for 3-4 hours. Refrigerate.

Concentrated Tea Method: Follow the manufacturers instructions.

Is your ice tea a little cloudy, add a small amount of boiling water.

ICED TEAS FLAVORED WITH ITALIAN STYLE SYRUPS

FOR A SINGLE SERVING OF FLAVORED ICE TEA

In a 16 oz. glass combine 1 oz. of Italian style syrup with 12 oz. of cold tea, fill remainder of glass with ice.

By using one of the prepared teas, you can create your own flavor combination or use one of the following.

Almond Iced Tea

2 *quarts cold tea, combined with* 1/3 *cup almond* Italian *style syrup.*

Amaretto Iced Tea

2 *quarts cold tea, combined with* 1/3 *cup amaretto* Italian *style syrup.*

Apricot Iced Tea

2 *quarts cold tea, combined with* 1/2 *cup apricot* Italian *style syrup.*

Bing Cherry Iced Tea

2 *quarts cold tea, combined with* 1/2 *cup black cherry* Italian *style syrup.*

Blackberry Iced Tea

2 *quarts cold tea, combined with* 1/2 *cup blackberry* Italian *style syrup.*

Boysenberry Iced Tea

2 *quarts cold tea, combined with* 1/2 *cup boysenberry* Italian *style syrup.*

Caramel Iced Tea

2 *quarts cold tea, combined with* 1/2 *cup caramel* Italian *style syrup.*

Cinnamon Iced Tea

2 *quarts cold tea, combined with* 1/2 *cup cinnamon* Italian *style syrup.*

Cherry Iced Tea

2 *quarts cold tea, combined with* 1/2 *cup cherry* Italian *style syrup.*

Cherry Nut Iced Tea

2 *quarts cold tea, combined with* 1/3 *cup cherry* Italian *style syrup and* 1/4 *cup almond* Italian *style syrup.*

Coconut Iced Tea

2 quarts cold tea, combined with 1/2 cup coconut Italian style syrup.

Cranberry Iced Tea

2 quarts cold tea, combined with 1/2 cup cranberry Italian style syrup.

Ginger Iced Tea

2 quarts cold tea, combined with 1/2 cup ginger Italian style syrup.

Ginger and Orange Iced Tea

2 quarts cold tea, combined with 1/4 cup ginger Italian style syrup and 1/4 cup orange Italian style syrup.

Grape Iced Tea

2 quarts cold tea, combined with 1/2 cup grape Italian style syrup.

Grape Berry Iced Tea

2 quarts cold tea, combined with 1/4 cup grape Italian style syrup and 1/4 cup blackberry Italian style syrup.

Kiwi Iced Tea

2 quarts cold tea, combined with 1/2 cup kiwi Italian style syrup.

Lemon Iced Tea

2 quarts cold tea, combined with 1/2 cup lemon Italian style syrup.

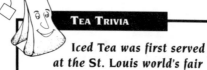

TEA TRIVIA

Iced Tea was first served at the St. Louis world's fair in 1904.

Mandarino Iced Tea
. . . .

2 quarts cold tea, combined with 1/2 cup mandarino Italian style syrup.

Mango Iced Tea
. . . .

2 quarts cold tea, combined with 1/2 cup mango Italian style syrup.

Marzipan Orange Iced Tea
. . . .

2 quarts cold tea, combined with 1/3 cup orange Italian style syrup and 1/4 cup amaretto Italian style syrup.

Melon Iced Tea
. . . .

2 quarts cold tea, combined with 1/2 cup melon Italian style syrup.

Mint Iced Tea
. . . .

2 quarts cold tea, combined with 1/2 cup mint Italian style syrup.

Orange Iced Tea
. . . .

2 quarts cold tea, combined with 1/2 cup orange Italian style syrup.

Passion Fruit Iced Tea
. . . .

2 quarts cold tea, combined with 1/2 cup passion fruit Italian style syrup.

Peach Iced Tea
. . . .

2 quarts cold tea, combined with 1/2 cup peach Italian style syrup.

Peach Nut Iced Tea
. . . .

2 quarts cold tea, combined with 1/3 cup peach Italian style syrup and 1/4 cup almond Italian style syrup.

Pineapple Iced Tea
. . . .

2 quarts cold tea, combined with 1/2 cup pineapple Italian style syrup.

Praline Iced Tea
. . . .

2 quarts cold tea, combined with 1/2 cup praline Italian style syrup.

Raspberry Iced Tea

2 *quarts cold tea, combined with 1/2 cup raspberry Italian style syrup.*

Raspberry and Coconut Iced Tea

2 *quarts cold tea, combined with 1/4 cup raspberry Italian style syrup and 1/4 cup coconut Italian style syrup.*

Raspberry Licorice Iced Tea

2 *quarts cold tea, combined with 1/4 cup raspberry Italian style syrup and 1/4 cup licorice Italian style syrup.*

Rum Iced Tea

2 *quarts cold tea, combined with 1/2 cup rum Italian style syrup.*

Sambuca Iced Tea

2 *quarts cold tea, combined with 1/2 cup sambuca Italian style syrup.*

Strawberry Iced Tea

2 *quarts cold tea, combined with 1/2 cup strawberry Italian style syrup.*

Tangarine Iced Tea

2 *quarts cold tea, combined with 1/2 cup tangarine Italian style syrup.*

Vanilla Iced Tea

2 *quarts cold tea, combined with 1/2 cup vanilla Italian style syrup.*

TEA TRIVIA

80% of the tea consumed in the United States is Iced.

180

HERBAL TEA

Herbal teas are not from the tea plant, and are not really teas at all. They are mixtures of many different herbs, roots and spices, that are then brewed into a tea like beverage.

Herbal Teana

Herb Tea

BREWING HERBAL TEA

Start with fresh cold water. Heat water in a tea kettle to a full rolling boil. Pour boiling water into the cup, directly over the tea bag. Let steep for 4 minutes, remove bag add sweetener or flavor.

HERBAL TEAS & ITALIAN STYLE SYRUPS

Suggested Combinations for an 8 oz. cup

If your herbal tea flavor is:	Combine with the suggested Italian style syrup:
Apple:	1/2 tsp. Apple Italian style syrup 3/4 tsp. Cinnamon Italian style syrup
Blackberry:	1 tsp. Blackberry Italian style syrup
Blackberry/Orange:	1 tsp. Orange Italian style syrup
Blackberry/Spice:	1/2 tsp. Blackberry Italian style syrup 1/2 tsp. Cinnamon Italian style syrup
Cinnamon:	1 tsp. Cinnamon Italian style syrup
Cinnamon:	1 tsp. Ginger Italian style syrup
Cranberry:	1 tsp. Cranberry Italian style syrup
Cranberry:	1 tsp. Cherry Italian style syrup
Cranberry:	1 tsp. Raspberry Italian style syrup
Fruit Nut:	1 tsp. Almond Italian style syrup
Lemon:	1 tsp. Lemon Italian style syrup
Licorice:	1 tsp. Sambuca or Licorice Italian style syrup
Orange:	1 tsp. Orange Italian style syrup
Orange:	1 tsp. Cinnamon Italian style syrup
Peach:	1 tsp. Peach Italian style syrup
Peach/Nut:	1 tsp. Almond Italian style syrup
Peppermint:	1 tsp. Peppermint Italian style syrup
Peppermint:	1 tsp. Cherry Italian style syrup

These are just a few suggested combinations, don't stop here. Try creating a combination of your own.

HERBAL TEANA TRIVIA

The licorice root is 50 times sweeter than sugar cane, and has no calories.

Licorice root tea has an anesthetizing effect that can help soothe sore throats and relieve coughs.

For a goodnights sleep, try drinking a cup of sleepytime tea sweetened with a little honey.

Black Elder, an old time treatment for fever when brewed into a herb tea.

Have a cold? Try a cup of mint herbal tea sweetened with a teaspoon of honey.

Want to relax? Try a cup of herbal tea that contains the herb "skullcap."

The method of collecting herbs from the wild is called "wildcrafting." To some herbalists, wildcrafted herbs are the most potent (medically speaking) because they have been harvested from their natural habitat. Blending herbs for teas should be done with one herb at a time. This method is known as "simpling."

RECIPE INDEX

. . . .

Espresso
. . . .

Americanos
. . . .

Basic Latté Combinations
. . . .

Nice 'n' Spicy &
A Bit Of Honey

Mocha Madness

Iced Mochas

Holiday Specials

White Chocolate
· ·

Steamers
· · · · · · · · · · · · · · · · · · · ·

Italian Sodas
· · · · · · · · · · · · · · · · · · ·

Italian Smoothies
· · · · · · · · · · · · · · · · · · ·

Miscellaneous Drinks

Granitas

Homestyle Granitas

Tea
· · · · · · · · · · · · · · · · ·

Iced Teas Flavored With Italian Style Syrups
· · · · · · · · · · · · · · · · ·

Herbal Tea
· · · · · · · · · · · · · ·

ORDERING INFORMATION

To order The Espresso Bartenders Guide please send $13.95 (+p&h).
To order Espresso Humor of the 90's please send $5.95 (+p&h).

Postage & Handling $3.50 (Canada $4.50). Will ship 1 or both items.

_____ copies $ _____ Total Enclosed

WA residents please include 8.2% sales tax.

Send money order or check to: Hooked On Espresso
                                  Department 1
                                  9200 160th St. SE
                                  Snohomish, WA 98290

Notes

Notes

Notes

Notes

Notes

Notes

Thank You!